I Believe In Miracles

Jerry Byler

JBM

Jerry Byler Ministries
PO Box 1618
Northport AL 35476

I Believe In Miracles

Jerry Byler

Scriptures quoted in this book are taken from the
King James Version of the Holy Bible
unless otherwise stated.

© Copyright 2011 Jerry Byler

All rights reserved. No part of this publication may be reproduced, stored in a retrieval system or transmitted in any form or by any means, electronic, mechanical, photocopying, recording or otherwise, without the written permission of the author. All book orders and correspondence should be directed to:

Jerry Byler ● PO Box 1618
Northport AL 35476 ● (205) 799-7418

DEDICATION

I want to thank my precious wife, Carol Ann, for her love, faith and support during our roller coaster ride together over life's hills and through life's valleys.

Even though she now resides in Heaven with Jesus, we had 30 wonderful years together. I know that I will see her again.

Thank you, honey, for waiting on me hand and foot during the recovery from my injuries sustained in the head-on collision, when I could not even raise my head from my pillow.

I will never forget you.

I will always love you.

ACKNOWLEDGEMENTS

I would like to thank God, the Father and the Lord Jesus Christ, for saving me and calling me into the ministry to work for Him and for opening doors and opportunities for me to teach His Word. Without Him, I could do nothing.

I want to thank my parents, Paul and Mary Byler, for being holy, righteous and God fearing people and for teaching me when I was a child in the ways of the Lord. Thank you Dad for being there for me and helping me many times. I love you very much.

I want to thank my daughter and son-in-law, Brent and Brandi Shirley, and my three precious grandchildren, Coy, Colby and Olivia Ann for bringing so much joy, happiness and laughter into my life when it seemed that I could never laugh again after my wife's passing.

I want to thank my sisters, Annette Messer and Lois and Sharon Byler for your love, kindness and generosity you have shown me my entire life.

I want to thank my brother-in-law, Reverend Donnie Messer, for my first preaching opportunity in church and for being the brother that I never had. And I thank my sweet, kind and loving niece, Melanie Messer, for all that you do. You are an inspiration to me. And thanks to my nephew, Donithin Messer, and his wife, Jessica.

And to the rest of my relatives and my wife's relatives, I love you and I pray that all will make it to Heaven so we can have a wonderful family reunion one day.

Contents

I Believe In Miracles!	7
Simply Believe	17
SOZO	21
Diasozo	33
The Healer & Redeemer	37
Speak The Word Only	43
Only Believe	51
Where Does Sickness And Disease Come From?	57
Understanding Sickness	71
Mustard Seed Faith	75
The Fig Tree	83
The Lord's Supper	89
The Children's Bread	93
The Name of Jesus	97
Who You Are In Christ	101
Your Words	111
How To Keep Your Healing	123
Catalog of Books, DVDs & Computer CDs	125

Chapter One

I Believe In Miracles!

July 29, 2002 is a day that I will never forget. As a salesman for a foodservice distributor, a customer called me that morning and said the truck shorted him a case of kale. Kale is a vegetable of the cabbage family but does not form a head as cabbage does. My customer was using kale to decorate his salad bar.

Since the warehouse was located adjacent to the city in which I lived, I drove to it, picked up a case of kale, put it in the back of my 1996 Ford Explorer and took it to my customer just a few miles away.

After delivering the kale to my customer, I drove across the street, filled my Explorer with gas and went up the ramp onto interstate highway 59, headed toward my first customer of the day 60 miles away.... or so I thought.

There was an exit to a major U.S. highway just a couple of miles down the interstate. It was approximately 8:00 am. Traffic was pretty heavy. There was a line of cars in the outside lane and I knew the majority of them would probably exit. I moved to the inside lane, as I would bypass the exit. I was going 70 mph.

A couple of minutes earlier, a car had come up the interstate exit ramp going the wrong way. Driving north in the southbound lane at 70 mph, the driver swerved to the inside lane to avoid colliding with the cars in the outside lane.

I didn't see him until he swerved into my lane. By then it was too late! We hit head-on immediately! I saw him for a split second and then... BAM!

The impact was tremendous... the same as hitting a brick wall at 140 mph! Upon impact, I thought, *"I'm dead!"*

Then, to my horror, my 1996 Ford Explorer rolled over and over and over and over, I don't know how many times! As my Explorer was rolling I thought, *"I know I'm dead now because nobody survives wrecks like this!"* And because I was expecting to die at any second, I said, *"Lord, take care of my family."*

I had heard about Ford Explorer rollovers, with many people being killed when their vehicle left the road and turned over. My Explorer had not only turned over, but was rolling and flipping multiple times down the interstate... after already being in a head on collision with an impact of 140 mph! There was no way someone could survive a wreck like this! Or could they?

Less than two years earlier, two prophets had spoken to me about the Lord having a work for me to do. I had submitted myself totally to the Lord and was eagerly anticipating the doors and opportunities to open for me to go into the ministry.

But now, as my vehicle was rolling and flipping down the interstate, I was trying to hold onto life with every ounce of strength. On the last roll, the roof of my Explorer caved in, hit me in the head and broke my neck!

Already, I had severely bit my tongue at the impact, the force being so tremendous. And my right foot was pinned under the dash since the motor was compressed by the impact.

When my Explorer finally quit rolling, it was on its side, driver side up and I was dangling in the air by the seatbelt. The first thing I said was, *"I'm alive! I'm alive!"* Somehow, I couldn't believe it! Tragically, the man who hit me was killed.

And then I noticed that my right side was completely numb... and that frightened me. I thought I was paralyzed on that side. But the numbness was due to two things... the first being, my chest put incredible force on the seatbelt as my body was lunging forward at the impact. That saved me from going though the windshield.

And secondly, as my vehicle was rolling and flipping multiple times, my chest was beating the steering wheel violently, even bending it! No wonder I was numb on my right side. And while my chest was beating the steering wheel, my extreme lower back was beating the console violently!

As I was hanging in the air by the seatbelt, I noticed smoke filling my Explorer. Several people had stopped and were looking in where the windshield used to be (it had been knocked out). Grimacing in almost unbearable pain, I managed to ask, *"Where is this smoke coming from?"*

Someone screamed, *"Oh man, your truck is on fire!"* I had just filled up with gas a few minutes earlier. I could envision my car exploding like they do in the movies. I did not want to burn alive. But I was trapped. The seatbelt would not release and my foot was pinned under the dash.

I begged for someone to stop people on the interstate and ask for a fire extinguisher. I did not want to burn!

Another person had just stopped, had a fire extinguisher and put the fire out! That was a miracle! Praise God for watching over me! How many people do you know who carry fire extinguishers in their car?

Since I was dangling in the air, the seatbelt was putting incredible pressure on my chest. I couldn't stand it any longer. The seatbelt was locked in crash mode and would not unhook. Finally, a man reached through where the windshield used to be and cut the seatbelt in two with his knife.

I fell from the driver's side to the passenger's side with my foot still pinned under the dash. It was July, hot and steaming! I was now between the passenger seat and floorboard for what seemed like thirty minutes although I'm sure it was less time.

Finally, the paramedics and ambulance arrived. They had to pry open the doors (they wouldn't open, being damaged) to get an opening to pull me out. They couldn't get my foot loose from under the dash at first; so several guys grabbed me and literally jerked my foot loose with all of their might! Finally, I was free of the car! (My foot came out of my shoe... my shoe remained under the dash).

My injuries were:

My neck was broken... The doctor said if it had broken just a fraction more toward the center, I would have been paralyzed from my neck down! I had to wear a neck brace for almost three months but praise God it healed with no surgery!

I had several broken ribs. They healed with no surgery and no complications.

My coccyx (commonly called the tailbone) was cracked. I couldn't sit down very long at a time for about a year. It also healed with no surgery and no complications.

My tongue was nearly bitten through at the impact! There was a big lump on it for months but it too healed completely!

My nose was infected for months from the airbag powder that was pounded into my face on the initial impact. But eventually, it healed too.

The hospital had to monitor my heart several days to make sure the force of the impact didn't damage it. Praise God, my heart was ok!

On the second day in the hospital, I was told that my right foot was crushed on the right side and that I would never walk on that foot again! I was devastated! I asked them to try what they could.

They put a cast on it and then the next week, they cut the cast off, made adjustments, put another cast on... and repeated that process every week for multiple weeks.

After two months, I was given a walking shoe and a couple of weeks later I put my regular shoes back on! I walked with a limp for about a year. But now, I walk normally with no limp and no surgeries! My foot healed completely! That was a miracle!

Everything healed with no surgeries, no complications and no permanent disabilities and I went back to work full time in only 90 days! Glory to God! That was another miracle!

Some of my customers said, *"From what we heard about you, we didn't expect you back for a year!"* Some didn't expect that I would ever be able to work again.

But I discovered something in all of this. You are invincible until your time is up! And we are promised 70 years (Psalm 90:10). Any more than that and you are truly blessed!

Of course we have to abide in Him and His Words must abide in us. Then we can ask what we will and we know we will have whatever we ask for!

Now, if escaping death by the hand of God wasn't amazing enough already, let me tell you about a truly exciting miracle that happened during the accident.

Approximately six months before the accident, my seatbelt had broken. That's right... it was broken! The button was pushed in all the way and it wouldn't 'click' or catch or hook or whatever you want to call it. You could pick it up, shake it and it would rattle. It was broken.

My wife told me, *"You had better get it fixed because as much as you drive, you never know what might happen."* But like most everyone, I procrastinated about getting it fixed.

However, by habit, I fasten my seatbelt everywhere I go even if it's just across the street. So even though my seatbelt was broken, I laid the seatbelt into the slot. I felt safer that way even though it wasn't fastened.

On most days, I laid the seatbelt into the slot thirty or more times. If I leaned forward just a little, the seatbelt would slide out of the hole and I would just slide it back in with my right hand. But it wouldn't 'click'. It wouldn't 'catch'. It was broken as broken could be.

Just before the accident happened, the seatbelt slid out of the slot and I slid it back in. Then...

BAM! The guy hit me head-on!

Lo and behold... That broken seatbelt held me at the initial 140 mph impact! That broken seatbelt held me while I was rolling and flipping multiple times down the interstate! And that broken seatbelt held me so good, it wouldn't come loose or unhooked and a man had to cut it in two with a knife!

That, my friends, is a miracle!!

But that's not the end of the story.

I received a settlement from the insurance company and wanted to do something good with it. I knew a man who had been a missionary for fifty years or so to Haiti, the poorest country on earth.

I discovered, through my Dad, that this missionary had an opportunity to hold a crusade in a remote, mountainous region of central Mexico where they had never heard the gospel! To bring in his equipment and missionary team would require several thousand dollars.

I felt strongly that the Lord wanted to use me in making this crusade happen. I wrote a check for half the amount the missionary needed and sent it along with a letter detailing my accident.

A couple of weeks later, the Lord convicted me of not sending the full amount the missionary needed. At the time, I had the money. So I sat down, wrote a check for the other half and in the letter, I said, *"This is the second half that I should have sent with the first half."*

A couple of weeks later, I received a letter from the missionary. He said, *"Brother Jerry, let me tell you what has happened! I told the Lord that if the crusade was going to happen, He would have to provide the money. I went to my mailbox and your first check was there! So I praised God!"*

"I took an airplane to Mexico, rented a van and drove to where the road ended. From there, we rode in the back of a wagon for hours until we reached the remote village. We met the village leaders, finalized all the arrangements for the crusade and rode for hours in the back of the wagon back to where the van was."

"When we got back to the van, vandals had stripped it completely. There was nothing left. We had personal equipment and belongings in the van and they were gone as well."

"Was I dejected! We had to catch a ride to the nearest town, a bus to the nearest city and a plane home. I thought I had made a mistake in hearing the voice of the Lord about the crusade."

"Arriving home, I went to the mailbox and behold, your second check was there! Praise God! Full steam ahead!"

This missionary had the crusade and he said it was one of his most successful! 1,200 people were saved and a woman got out of her wheelchair and walked for the first time!

And since the door had been opened, he went back the following year and another 1,200 people were saved!

So as a result of the devil trying to kill me in the head-on collision, 2,400 people were saved!! I give God all the glory!! Praise His Holy Name!!

A few years later, I felt led of the Lord to study healings and miracles in the Bible. For the next several weeks, my evenings were consumed with the Bible, studying the Scriptures.

The result of my study is found in the following chapters of this book.

If you, a loved one, or someone you know needs healing or a miracle, then I pray that this book will build your faith in order to receive what you need from the Lord.

Chapter Two

Simply Believe

Did you know that you could receive healing as easily as salvation? It's true and by the time you get through reading this book, you will know the real truth about divine healing and the truth will make you free. (John 8:32)

To be saved, do what Romans 10:9-10 says:

> That if thou shalt confess with thy mouth the Lord Jesus, and shalt believe in thine heart that God hath raised him from the dead, thou shalt be saved.
> For with the heart man believeth unto righteousness; and with the mouth confession is made unto salvation.
> (Romans 10:9-10)

You are saved by confessing and BELIEVING what you confessed.

> For God so loved the world, that he gave his only begotten Son, that WHOSOEVER BELIEVETH IN HIM should not perish, but have everlasting life.
> (John 3:16)

Ephesians 2:8 says:

> For by grace are ye saved through faith;
> (Ephesians 2:8)

If you have faith, you believe. If you believe, you have faith.

So the key to being saved is to SIMPLY BELIEVE what you confess!

Likewise, the key to being healed is to also SIMPLY BELIEVE what you confess!

That's because salvation and healing go hand in hand. When you receive one, you can receive the other automatically! When you receive salvation, you can also receive healing by simply confessing and believing for it. When you receive healing, you can also receive salvation by simply confessing and believing for it.

The two are inseparable! This is the TOTAL PACKAGE or the great redemption plan of God for mankind that few people understand!

When Jesus died for our sins, He gave us a two-fold redemption; (1) By His precious blood He shed on the cross for our sins, we receive forgiveness of sins or salvation; and (2) With His stripes He took upon His body, we receive healing (we are healed). Isaiah 53:5 says:

> But he was wounded for our transgression, he was bruised for our iniquities: the chastisement of our peace was upon him; and with his stripes we are healed. (Isaiah 53:5)

Matthew 8:17 says that Jesus Himself TOOK OUR INFIRMITIES, and BARE OUR SICKNESSES.

Why do you continue to bear sickness and disease in your body when Jesus has already taken them and bared them for you!

What Jesus has already bared... you don't have to! Rebuke that sickness in the Name of Jesus and command it to leave your body at once!

When God planned redemption for mankind, He thought of <u>everything</u> that we would ever need to have COMPLETE and TOTAL VICTORY over the devil and his evil plans for us. In fact, it's hard for human reasoning to understand the awesomeness of God's love for us!

The Apostle Paul says in Ephesians 3:17-19:

> That Christ may dwell in your hearts by faith; that ye, being rooted and grounded in love,
> May be able to comprehend with all saints what is the breadth, and length, and depth, and height;
> And to know the love of Christ, which passeth knowledge, that ye might be filled with all the fullness of God.
> (Ephesians 3:17-19)

Ephesians 1:22 says Jesus *hath put ALL THINGS under His feet,* and that INCLUDES sickness, disease, depression, fear, worry, and more! Glory to His Holy Name!

All we need to do is SIMPLY BELIEVE that Jesus <u>HAS ALREADY</u> put ALL THINGS under His feet (just as the Bible declares) and PRAISE GOD FOR THE VICTORY instead of living in despair!

Chapter Three

SOZO

Do you still need MORE proof that Jesus gave us a two-fold or DOUBLE redemption? Do you need MORE proof that you can be healed as easily as you can be saved? Okay, brothers and sisters, read on!

The Greek word 'SOZO' (pronounced sōde'-zō) is defined by the Greek dictionary as TO SAVE, DELIVER, PROTECT, HEAL, and BE MADE WHOLE.

Notice that both SALVATION and HEALING are included in the definition above!

Now, read all of the following salvation and healing Scriptures that had the Greek word 'SOZO' in the original manuscripts. They are ALL very important... don't skip any of them. Read them slowly and meditate on what they are actually saying. For emphasis, I have capitalized and underlined the translated English word in each Scripture that was originally 'SOZO'.

My reference is *Strong's Exhaustive Concordance of the Bible,* which also contains the *Greek Dictionary* of *the New Testament.*

And she shall bring forth a son, and thou shalt call his name JESUS: for he shall <u>SAVE</u> his people from their sins.
(Matthew 1:21)

For the Son of man is come to <u>SAVE</u> that which was lost. (Matthew 18:11)

For the Son of man is not come to destroy men's lives, but to <u>SAVE</u> them.
(Luke 9:56)

And if any man hear my words, and believe not, I judge him not: for I came not to judge the world, but to <u>SAVE</u> the world.
(John 12:47)

And with many other words did he testify and exhort, saying, <u>SAVE</u> yourselves from this untoward (crooked) generation.
(Acts 2:40)

For I speak to you Gentiles, inasmuch as I am the apostle of the Gentiles, I magnify mine office:
If by any means I may provoke to emulation (jealously), them which are my flesh, and might <u>SAVE</u> same of them.
(Romans 11:13-14)

For after that in the wisdom of God the world by wisdom knew not God, it pleased God by the foolishness of preaching to <u>SAVE</u> them that believe.
(I Corinthians 1:21)

For what knowest thou, O wife, whether thou shalt <u>SAVE</u> thy husband? Or how knowet thou, O man, whether thou shalt SAVE thy wife?

But as God hath distributed to every man, as the Lord hath called every one, so let him walk... (1 Corinthians 7:16-17)

To the weak became I as weak, that I might gain the weak: I am made all things to all men, that I might by all means SAVE some. (I Corinthians 9:22)

This is a faithful saying, and worthy of all acceptation, that Christ Jesus came into the world to SAVE sinners; of whom I am chief. (I Timothy 1:15)

Take heed unto thyself, and unto the doctrine; continue in them: for in doing this thou shalt both SAVE thyself, and them that hear thee. (I Timothy 4:16)

Wherefore he (Jesus) is able also to SAVE them to the uttermost that come unto God by him, seeing he ever liveth to make intercession for them. (Hebrews 7:25)

Wherefore lay apart all filthiness and superfluity (excess) of naughtiness, and receive with meekness the engrafted (planted) word, which is able to SAVE your souls. (James 1:21)

What doth it profit, my brethren, though a man say he hath faith, and have not works? Can faith SAVE him? (James 2:14)

And the prayer of faith shall SAVE (HEAL) the sick, and the Lord shall raise him up; and if he have committed sins, they shall be forgiven him. (James 5:15)

Let him know, that he which converteth the sinner from the error of his way, shall SAVE a soul from death, and shall hide a multitude of sins. (James 5:20)

And ye shall be hated of all men for my name's sake: but he that endureth to the end shall be SAVED. (Matthew 10:22)

And again I say unto you, It is easier for a camel to go through the eye of a needle, than for a rich man to enter into the kingdom of God.

When his disciples heard it, they were exceedingly amazed, saying, Who then can be SAVED? (Matthew 19:24-25)

And many false prophets shall arise, and shall deceive many.
And because iniquity shall abound, the love of many shall wax cold.
But he that shall endure unto the end, the same shall be SAVED.
(Matthew 24:11-13)

It is easier for a camel to go through the eye of a needle, than for a rich man to enter in to the kingdom of God.

And they were astonished out of measure, saying among themselves, Who then can be SAVED? (Mark 10:25-26)

He that believeth and is baptized shall be SAVED: (Mark 16:16)

And he said to the woman, Thy faith hath SAVED thee; (Luke 7:50)

Now the parable is this: The seed is the word of God.

Those by the way side are they that hear; then cometh the devil, and taketh away the word out of their hearts, lest they should believe and be SAVED.
(Luke 8:11-12)

For God sent not his Son into the world to condemn the world; but that the world through him might be SAVED. (John 3:17)

But these things I say, that ye might be SAVED. (John 5:34)

I am the door; by me if any man enter in, he shall be SAVED, (John 10:9)

And it shall come to pass, that whosoever shall call on the name of the Lord shall be SAVED. (Acts 2:21)

And the Lord added to the church daily such as should be SAVED. (Acts 2:47)

Neither is there salvation in any other: for there is none other name under heaven given among men, whereby we must be SAVED. (Acts 4:12)

Send men to Joppa, and call for Simon, whose surname is Peter;
Who shall tell thee words, whereby thou and all thy house shall be SAVED.
(Acts 11:13-14)

But we believe that through the grace of the Lord Jesus Christ, we shall be <u>SAVED</u>,
(Acts 15:11)

Then he called for a light, and sprang in, and came trembling, and fell down before Paul and Silas,

And brought them out, and said, Sirs, what must I do to be <u>SAVED</u>?

And they said, Believe on the Lord Jesus Christ, and thou shalt be <u>SAVED</u>, and thy house. (Acts 16:29-31)

That if thou shalt confess with thy mouth the Lord Jesus, and shalt believe in thine heart that God hath raised him from the dead, thou shalt be <u>SAVED</u>.

For with the heart man believeth unto righteousness; and with the mouth confession is made unto salvation.
(Romans 10:9-10)

For whosoever shall call upon the name of the Lord shall be <u>SAVED</u>.
(Romans 10:13)

For the preaching of the cross is to them that perish foolishness; but unto us which are <u>SAVED</u> it is the power of God.
(I Corinthians 1:18)

Even as I please all men in all things, not seeking mine own profit, but the profit of many, that they may be <u>SAVED</u>.
(I Corinthians 10:33)

(By grace ye are <u>SAVED</u>;)
(Ephesians 2:5)

SOZO 27

> For by grace are ye SAVED through faith; (Ephesians 2:8)

> For this is good and acceptable in the sight of God our Saviour;
> Who will have all men to be SAVED, and to come unto the knowledge of the truth. (I Timothy 2:3-4)

> Who hath SAVED us, and called us with an holy calling, not according to our works, but according to his own purpose and grace, which was given us in Christ Jesus before the world began, (II Timothy 1:9)

> Not by works of righteousness which we have done, but according to his mercy he SAVED us, (Titus 3:5)

Now, after reading these Scriptures, do you have any doubt that the words SAVE and SAVED (used in these Scriptures and translated from the Greek word SOZO), means SALVATION and FORGIVENESS OF SINS?

Do you really believe that? Good. Let's move on and read some other Scriptures.

> And behold, there cometh one of the rulers of the synagogue, Jairus by name; and when he saw him (Jesus), he fell at his feet,
> And besought him greatly, saying, My little daughter lieth at the point of death: I pray thee, come and lay thy hands on her, that she may be HEALED: and she shall live. (Mark 5:22-23)
> Then they went out to see what was done; and came to Jesus, and found the

man, out of whom the devils were departed, sitting at the feet of Jesus clothed, and in his right mind: and they were afraid.

They also which saw it told them by what means he was possessed of the devils was <u>HEALED</u>. (Luke 8:35-36)

And there sat a certain man at Lystra, impotent in his feet, being a cripple from his mother's womb, who never had walked:

The same heard Paul speak: who stedfastly beholding him, and perceiving that he had faith to be <u>HEALED</u>,

Said with a loud voice, Stand upright on thy feet. And he leaped and walked.
(Acts 14:8-10)

And, behold, a woman, which was diseased with an issue of blood twelve years, came behind him, and touched the hem of his garments:

For she said within herself, If I may but touch his garment, I shall be <u>WHOLE</u>.

But Jesus turned him about, and when he saw her, he said, Daughter, be of good comfort; thy faith hath made thee <u>WHOLE</u>. And the woman was made <u>WHOLE</u> from that hour. (Matthew 9:20-22)

For she said, If I may touch but his clothes, I shall be <u>WHOLE</u>.

And straightway the fountain of her blood was dried up; and she felt in her body that she was healed of that plague.
(Mark 5:28-29)

And he (Jesus) said unto her, Daughter, thy faith hath made thee <u>WHOLE</u>;
(Mark 5:34)

And whithersoever he (Jesus) entered, into villages, or cities, or country, they laid the sick in the streets, and besought him that they might touch if it were but the border of his garment: and as many as touched him were made <u>WHOLE</u>.
(Mark 6:56)

And Jesus answered and said unto him (blind Bartimaeus), What wilt thou that I should do unto thee? The blind man said unto him, Lord, that I might receive my sight.
And Jesus said unto him, Go thy way; thy faith hath made thee <u>WHOLE</u>. And immediately he received his sight,
(Mark 10:51-52)

And he (Jesus) said unto her (woman with the issue of blood), Daughter be of good comfort: thy faith hath made thee <u>WHOLE</u>; (Luke 8:48)

But when Jesus heard it (Jairus' daughter being dead), he answered him, saying, Fear not: believe only, and she shall be made <u>WHOLE</u>. (Luke 8:50)

And (Jesus) took her by the hand, and called, saying, Maid, arise.
And her spirit came again, and she arose straightway: (Luke 54-55)

> And Jesus answering said, Were there not ten (lepers) cleansed? but where are the nine?
>
> There are not found that returned to give glory to God, save (except) this stranger.
>
> And he said unto him, Arise, go thy way: thy faith hath made thee <u>WHOLE</u>.
>
> (Luke 17:17-19)
>
> Then Peter, filled with the Holy Ghost, said unto them, Ye rulers of the people, and elders of Israel,
>
> If we this day be examined of the good deed done to the impotent man (the lame man at the temple gate Beautiful), by what means he is made <u>WHOLE</u>.
>
> Be it known unto you all, and to all the people of Israel, that by the name of Jesus Christ of Nazareth, whom ye crucified, whom God raised from the dead, even by him doth this man stand here before you <u>WHOLE</u>. (Acts 4:8-10)

Now, after reading these Scriptures, do you have any doubt that the words HEALED and WHOLE (used in these Scriptures and <u>translated from the Greek word SOZO</u>) means HEALING and RESTORED HEALTH?

Now, listen very carefully...

All four words (SAVE, SAVED, HEALED and WHOLE) were translated from the SAME Greek word 'SOZO' from the ORIGINAL MANUSCRIPTS!

You can check this out yourself by looking in *Strong's Exhaustive Concordance* of *the Bible* that is the authority in Scripture accuracy!

THIS PROVES THAT <u>JESUS GAVE US A TWO-FOLD OR DOUBLE REDEMPTION</u> AND THAT WE CAN RECEIVE BOTH SPIRITUAL AND PHYSICAL HEALING!

Where the Bible talks about salvation, it is also talking about healing. Where the Bible talks about healing, it is also talking about salvation. That's because the two are inseparable!

This is a Biblical fact! Jesus has already provided it for us! You can receive healing as easily as salvation! All you have to do is <u>SIMPLY BELIEVE</u>!

Chapter Four

Diasozo

DIASOZO, pronounced dee-as-odze'-o is the word SOZO prefixed with dia (pronounced dee-ah'). The definition is the same except DIA places a stronger emphasis on the act.

Since SOZO's definition is 'to save' and 'to heal' or 'make whole', DIASOZO's definition is: TO SAVE THROUGHLY and to MAKE PERFECTLY WHOLE! It also means to keep SAFE and to ESCAPE! Praise God!

Notice that DIASOZO means not just to save us but save us THROUGHLY! Notice that DIASOZO means not just to heal us but make us PERFECTLY whole! Again, this proves that Jesus gave us a two-fold or double redemption!

Now, read the following Scriptures that had the Greek word 'DIASOZO' in the original manuscripts. For emphasis, I have capitalized and underlined the translated English word in each Scripture that was originally 'DIASOZO'.

> And when the men of that place had knowledge, of him (Jesus), they sent out into all that country round about, and brought unto him all that were diseased;

And besought him that they might only touch the hem of his garment and as many as touched were <u>MADE PERFECTLY WHOLE</u>. (Matthew 14:35-36)

And a certain centurion's servant, who was dear unto him, was sick, and ready to die.

And when he heard of Jesus, he sent unto him the elders of the Jews, beseeching him that he would come and <u>HEAL</u> his servant. (Luke 7:2-3)

And he called unto him two centurions, saying, Make ready two hundred soldiers to go to Caesarea, and horsemen threescore and ten, and spearmen two hundred, at the third hour of the night;

And provide them beasts, that they may set Paul on, and bring him <u>SAFE</u> unto Felix the governor. (Acts 23:23-24)

But the centurion, willing <u>TO SAVE</u> Paul, kept them from their purpose; and commanded that they which could swim should cast themselves first into the sea, and get to land:

And the rest, some on boards, and some on broken pieces of the ship. And so it came to pass, that they <u>ESCAPED ALL SAFE</u> to land. (Acts 27:43-44)

And when they were <u>ESCAPED</u>, then they knew that the island was called Melita. (Acts 28:1)

And when the barbarians saw the venomous beast hang on his hand, they said among themselves, No doubt this man is a murderer, whom, though he hath <u>ESCAPED</u> the sea, yet vengeance suffereth not to live. (Acts 28:4)

For Christ also hath once suffered for sins, the just for the unjust, that he might bring us to God, being put to death in the flesh, but quickened by the Spirit:
By which also he went and preached unto the spirits in prison;
Which sometime were disobedient, when once the longsuffering of God waited in the days of Noah, while the ark was a preparing, wherein few, that is, eight souls were <u>SAVED</u> by water. (I Peter 3:18-20)

Glory to God! Now, is there any doubt that Jesus gave us a TWO-FOLD or DOUBLE redemption? Now, do you see that by Jesus' precious blood He shed that YOU can receive FORGIVENESS OF SINS and that with His stripes YOU can receive HEALING?

Now, do you see that YOU can receive HEALING as easily as salvation? All you have to do SIMPLY BELIEVE!

Chapter Five

The Healer & Redeemer

When you receive Jesus Christ into your heart, you receive the HEALER as well as the SAVIOR!

Exodus 15:26 says, ... *I am the Lord that healeth thee.*

In Exodus 3:14, when Moses asked God's Name, the Lord answered: *I AM THAT I AM.*

Since God is the great I AM, Exodus 15:26 (in my opinion) should be read like this:

I AM, the Lord that healeth thee.

Instead of reading this Scripture as if the Lord is simply making a statement, I believe it should be read as though the Lord is giving us a PERSONAL GUARANTEE that He WILL heal us!

It's the same as if I would say: Jerry Byler, the man who will teach God's Word.

This is more than a statement. It is my personal guarantee that I WILL teach God's Word and do whatever the Lord wants me to do.

By the way, I am using this as an illustration ONLY to help you understand this teaching. I am in NO way referencing myself on the same level as God Almighty. As a child of God, I am His son carrying on the family business.

God says: I AM, the Lord who healeth thee (or) I AM, the Lord who heals YOU!

You can take it to the bank... when God promises you anything He is faithful to perform His Word (Ezekiel 12:25). You just need faith to BELIEVE His Word and ACT on it!

God's Word is the dynamite... your faith is the fuse. You light the fuse by believing God's Word and acting out your faith. The result is an EXPLOSION of God's Power that surges throughout your body and healing is the result! Read that again and again!

David wrote in Psalms 103:2-3:

> **Bless the Lord, O my soul, and forget not ALL his benefits:**
> **Who FORGIVETH ALL thine iniquities (sin); who HEALETH ALL thy diseases;**
> (Psalms 103:2-3)

Did you know that as Christians, we have benefits? Just as you may have benefits at your job, Christians have benefits too! Forgiveness of sin, healing, provision, protection, peace, joy, and eternal life are all wonderful benefits we can enjoy!

Jesus is also our Redeemer. The Holy Spirit through the Apostle Paul says in Galatians 3:13:

> Christ hath redeemed us from the curse of the law, being made a curse for us: for it is written, Cursed is every one that hangeth on a tree: (Galatians 3:13)

What curse?

In Deuteronomy 28:15, God says:

> But it shall come to pass, if thou wilt not hearken unto the voice of the Lord thy God, to observe to do all his commandments and his statutes which I command thee this day; that all these curses shall come upon thee, and overtake thee: (Deuteronomy 28:15)

Then God lists in Deuteronomy 28:16-68 all the diseases that will come upon people who sin against Him. Read this chapter in Deuteronomy. These curses cover EVERY DISEASE known or unknown! If your sickness or disease is not specifically mentioned, then the following covers it (this is still God talking):

> If thou wilt not observe to do all the words of this law that are written in this book, that thou mayest fear this glorious and fearful name THE LORD THY GOD;
>
> Then the Lord will make thy plagues wonderful, and the plagues of thy seed, even great plagues, and of long continuance, and sore sicknesses, and of long continuance.
>
> Moreover he will bring upon thee all the diseases of Egypt, which thou wast afraid of; and they shall cleave unto thee.
>
> Also EVERY SICKNESS, and EVERY PLAGUE, which is not written in the book of

this law, them will the Lord bring upon thee, until thou be destroyed.

(Deuteronomy 28:58-61)

EVERY sickness and EVERY plague covers EVERYTHING doesn't it? Even generational curses are mentioned (the plagues of thy seed).

But Jesus took upon Himself ALL our infirmities, ALL our sicknesses, ALL our diseases, ALL our sins and He has REDEEMED us from the curse of the law! Praise God!

If you have cancer, say out loud: *"Deuteronomy 28 says that cancer is a curse of the law, but praise God, Galatians 3:13 says that Jesus has redeemed me from the curse of the law, therefore, cancer has no right to exist in my body and must leave in the Name of Jesus. Halleluiah!"*

If you have heart disease, say out loud: *"Deuteronomy 28 says that heart disease is a curse of the law, but praise God, Galatians 3:13 says that Jesus has redeemed me from the curse of the law, therefore, heart disease has no right to exist in my body and must leave in the Name of Jesus. Halleluiah!"*

If you suffer with migraine headaches, say out loud: *"Deuteronomy 28 says that migraine headaches is a curse of the law, but praise God, Galatians 3:13 says that Jesus has redeemed me from the curse of the law, therefore, migraine headaches have no right to exist in my body and must leave in the Name of Jesus. Halleluiah!"*

If you have ulcers, say out loud: *"Deuteronomy 28 says that ulcers is a curse of the law, but praise God, Galatians 3:13 says that Jesus has redeemed me from the curse of the law, therefore, ulcers have no right to exist in my body and must leave in the Name of Jesus. Halleluiah!"*

If you have any kind of tumor, say out loud: *"Deuteronomy 28 says that tumors are a curse of the law, but praise God, Galatians 3:13 says that Jesus has redeemed me from the curse of the law, therefore, tumors have no right to exist in my body and must leave in the Name of Jesus. Halleluiah!"*

If you suffer with back pain, say out loud: *"Deuteronomy 28 says that back pain is a curse of the law, but praise God, Galatians 3:13 says that Jesus has redeemed me from the curse of the law, therefore, back pain has no right to exist in my body and must leave in the Name of Jesus. Halleluiah!"*

If you have a blood disease or high blood pressure or high cholesterol, say out loud: *"Deuteronomy 28 says that blood disease (or high blood pressure or high cholesterol) is a curse of the law, but praise God, Galatians 3:13 says that Jesus has redeemed me from the curse of the law, therefore, blood disease (or high blood pressure or high cholesterol) has no right to exist in my body and must leave in the Name of Jesus. Halleluiah!"*

If you have asthma or emphysema or any lung disorder, say out loud: *"Deuteronomy 28 says that asthma (or emphysema or a lung disorder) is a curse of the law, but praise God, Galatians 3:13 says that Jesus has redeemed me from the curse of the law, therefore, asthma (or emphysema or a lung disorder) has no right to exist in my body and must leave in the Name of Jesus. Halleluiah!"*

Do you get the picture? Say the sickness or disease afflicting YOU...OUT LOUD when repeating this phrase. By saying it over and over and over, out loud, it's just like taking medicine; only this is God's medicine, His Word!

Your ears will hear what you say and go down into your spirit. Eventually, by continuing to take God's medicine by quoting His Word, you will begin to BELIEVE what you say and when you BELIEVE what you say, that's when physical healing will take place!

It doesn't make any difference what sickness or disease you may have, big or little, almost well or almost dead, God's Word will work if you SIMPLY BELIEVE!

Chapter Six

Speak The Word Only

> And when Jesus was entered into Capernaum, there came unto him a centurion, beseeching him,
>
> And saying, Lord, my servant lieth at home sick of the palsy, grievously tormented.
>
> And Jesus saith unto him, I will come and heal him.
>
> The centurion answered and said, Lord, I am not worthy that thou shouldest come under my roof: but speak the word only, and my servant shall be healed.
>
> For I am a man under authority, having soldiers under me: and I say to this man, Go, and he goeth; and to another, Come, and he cometh; and to my servant, Do this, and he doeth it.
>
> When Jesus heard it, he marvelled, and said to them that followed, Verily I say unto you, I have not found so great faith, no, not in Israel. (Matthew 8:5-10)

When the centurion came to Jesus and told Him that one of his servants was at home sick of the palsy, notice the reply by Jesus: *I will come and heal him.*

Most people today know that Jesus is ABLE to heal but many don't know if He WILL heal today. Jesus stated His will in verse 7: *I will come and heal him.*

> When he was come down from the mountain, great multitudes followed him.
> And, behold, there came a leper and worshipped him, saying, Lord, if thou wilt, thou canst make me clean.
> And Jesus put forth his hand, and touched him, saying, I WILL; be thou clean. And immediately his leprosy was cleansed.
> (Matthew 8:1-3)

Again, Jesus said, *I will.* No mistake about it... it IS God's will for you to be healed.

Now, when Jesus told the centurion that He would come and heal his servant, notice the reply by the centurion:

> The centurion answered and said, Lord, I am not worthy that thou shouldest come under my roof: but speak the word only, and my servant shall be healed.
> For I am a man under authority, having soldiers under me: and I say to this man, Go, and he goeth; and to another, Come, and he cometh; and to my servant, Do this, and he doeth it. (Matthew 8:8-9)

What was the centurion saying? He was saying that he understood authority.

The centurion was saying, *"I am a man of authority. I say to one of my soldiers 'come' and he comes. I tell another soldier 'go' and he goes. I tell another soldier to 'do this' and he does it. My authority commands them and they obey my command."*

"And just as I am a man of authority over soldiers, you Jesus, are a man of authority over sickness, disease and demons. Just as my word of command gets action, Jesus, your Word of command also gets action."

"So, speak the Word only, and my servant will be healed! Just speak the Word only and that palsy must obey your command. It shall be done because I understand authority."

And when Jesus heard what the centurion said, verse 10 says that Jesus marveled or was amazed, and said, *Verily I say unto you, I have not found so great faith, no, not in Israel.*

Jesus said this centurion man, who was a Gentile, had more faith than any of the Covenant people or the Jews, in all of Israel!

Why? Because the centurion understood authority and he understood the authority that Jesus had... authority over sickness, disease and demons.

But really, Jesus has authority over all things because Jesus is the Living Word who created everything so the Word of God has creative authority or you can say it another way... that the Word of God has creative power!

If Jesus was to appear in my home church today, physically, and say, *"My, you have some nice green chairs."*

We would say, *"But Lord, they are not green, they are blue."*

But what you need to understand is… if Jesus said that the blue chairs were green, they would INSTANTLY turn green because the Word of God has creative power!

Let's look at another Scripture.

Now, after fasting for forty days and nights in the wilderness, the Bible says that Jesus was hungry. Then the devil comes to Jesus and tempts Him.

> And the devil, taking him up into an high mountain, shewed unto him all the kingdoms of the world in a moment of time.
> And the devil said unto him, All this power will I give thee, and the glory of them: for that is delivered unto me; and to whomsoever I will I give it.
> If thou therefore wilt worship me, all shall be thine. (Luke 4:5-7)

Where did the devil get this power? When man sinned in the Garden of Eden, satan became the god of the world. That's why he said, *All this power will I give thee, and the glory of them: for that is delivered unto me; and to whomsoever I will I give it. If thou therefore wilt worship me, all shall be thine.*

Of course, in Matthew 4:10, *Jesus answered and said unto him, Get thee behind me, Satan: for it is written, Thou shalt worship the Lord thy God, and him only shalt thou serve.*

And when Jesus shed His precious Holy blood on the cross and died, Colossians 2:15 says that Jesus *having spoiled principalities and powers, he made a shew of them openly, triumphing over them in it.*

The New Living translation says Jesus *disarmed the spiritual rulers and authorities.*

The Message version of the Bible says Jesus *stripped all the spiritual tyrants in the universe of their authority.*

Because of the shedding of His precious blood on the cross, and by His death, burial and resurrection, Jesus legally and forever more, repossessed and took back the power and authority that satan got at the fall of man.

> And Jesus came and spake unto them, saying, All power is given unto me in heaven and in earth.
> Go ye therefore, and teach all nations, baptizing them in the name of the Father, and of the Son, and of the Holy Ghost:
> (Matthew 28:18-19)

When Jesus said, *Go ye therefore...* He delegated or gave or handed over His power and authority to the Church.

And the Church has access to this power and authority in the Name of Jesus. Because when we use the Name of Jesus in dealing with sickness, disease and demons, it's as though Jesus is there doing it Himself. And you know when Jesus is there, the work is done!

> And he said unto them, Go ye into all the world, and preach the gospel to every creature.
> He that believeth and is baptized shall be saved; but he that believeth not shall be damned.

> And these signs shall follow them that believe; In my name shall they cast out devils; they shall speak with new tongues;
>
> They shall take up serpents; and if they drink any deadly thing, it shall not hurt them; they shall lay hands on the sick, and they shall recover.
>
> So then after the Lord had spoken unto them, he was received up into heaven, and sat on the right hand of God.
>
> And they went forth, and preached every where, the Lord working with them, and confirming the word with signs following. Amen. (Mark 16:15-20)

The Apostle Paul explains this in Ephesians 1:19-23:

> And what is the exceeding greatness of his power to us-ward who believe, according to the working of his mighty power,
>
> Which he wrought in Christ, when he raised him from the dead, and set him at his own right hand in the heavenly places,
>
> Far above all principality, and power, and might, and dominion, and every name that is named, not only in this world, but also in that which is to come:
>
> And hath put all things under his feet, and gave him to be the head over all things to the church,
>
> Which is his body, the fulness of him that filleth all in all. (Ephesians 1:19-23)

Jesus stripped satan of the power and authority he got at the fall of man in the Garden of Eden... and handed over that power and authority to the Church which we use in the Name of Jesus.

So take your place in the Family as a child of God and speak the Word only: *"With his stripes I am healed!"*

Speak the Word only: *"He is the LORD that heals me!"*

Speak the Word only: *"Himself took my infirmity, and bare my sickness."*

Speak the Word only: *"I am the head and not the tail, I will be above only and not be beneath."*

Speak the Word only: *"No weapon that is formed against me shall prosper."*

Speak the Word only: *"My God shall supply all of my need according to His riches in glory by Christ Jesus."*

Speak the Word only: *"I've never seen the righteous forsaken nor his seed begging bread."*

Speak the Word only: *"A thousand shall fall at my side, and ten thousand at my right hand; but it shall not come near me."*

Speak the Word only: *"In all my ways I will acknowledge Him and He will direct my paths."*

Speak the Word only: *"The Lord is my Shepherd, I shall not want."*

So whatever you need, whatever mountain is coming against you, speak the Word only... speak the Word only... with faith... and you shall have what you say!

Just speak the Word only!

Chapter Seven

Only Believe

And, behold, there cometh one of the rulers of the synagogue, Jairus by name; and when he saw him, he fell at his feet,

And besought him greatly, saying, My little daughter lieth at the point of death: I pray thee, come and lay thy hands on her, that she may be healed; and she shall live. (Mark's version of this story says that the little girl was twelve years old.)

And Jesus went with him; and much people followed him, and thronged him.

And a certain woman, which had an issue of blood twelve years,

And had suffered many things of many physicians, and had spent all that she had, and was nothing bettered, but rather grew worse,

When she had heard of Jesus, came in the press behind, and touched his garment.

For she said, If I may touch but his clothes, I shall be whole.

And straightway the fountain of her blood was dried up; and she felt in her body that she was healed of that plague.

> And Jesus, immediately knowing in himself that virtue had gone out of him, turned him about in the press, and said, Who touched my clothes?
>
> And his disciples said unto him, Thou seest the multitude thronging thee, and sayest thou, Who touched me?
>
> And he looked round about to see her that had done this thing.
>
> But the woman fearing and trembling, knowing what was done in her, came and fell down before him, and told him all the truth.
>
> And he said unto her, Daughter, thy faith hath made thee whole; go in peace, and be whole of thy plague.
>
> While he yet spake, there came from the ruler of the synagogue's house certain which said, Thy daughter is dead: why troublest thou the Master any further?
>
> (Mark 5:22-35)

In Jairus' mind, he may have said, *"Only if that woman hadn't come along and distracted Jesus, Jesus would have made it to my house on time and my little girl would not have died. But now, they say she is dead."*

> As soon as Jesus heard the word that was spoken, he saith unto the ruler of the synagogue, Be not afraid, ONLY BELIEVE.
>
> (Mark 5:36)

Only believe! There is always hope if you only believe! Dreams can be re-birthed if you only believe! As long as you are breathing, there is still hope; it can still come to pass... if you only believe!

Let's look at another Scripture.

> Now a certain man was sick, named Lazarus, of Bethany, the town of Mary and her sister Martha.
>
> (It was that Mary which anointed the Lord with ointment, and wiped his feet with her hair, whose brother Lazarus was sick.)
>
> Therefore his sisters sent unto him, saying, Lord, behold, he whom thou lovest is sick.
>
> When Jesus heard that, he said, This sickness is not unto death, but for the glory of God, that the Son of God might be glorified thereby.
>
> Now Jesus loved Martha, and her sister, and Lazarus.
>
> When he had heard therefore that he was sick, he abode two days still in the same place where he was. (John 11:1-6)

> (Jesus said) Our friend Lazarus sleepeth; but I go, that I may awake him out of sleep.
>
> Then said his disciples, Lord, if he sleep, he shall do well.
>
> Howbeit Jesus spake of his death: but they thought that he had spoken of taking of rest in sleep.
>
> Then said Jesus unto them plainly, Lazarus is dead.
>
> And I am glad for your sakes that I was not there, to the intent ye may believe; nevertheless let us go unto him. (John 11:11-15)

Then when Jesus came, he found that he had lain in the grave four days already.
(John 11:17)

Then Martha, as soon as she heard that Jesus was coming, went and met him: but Mary sat still in the house.

Then said Martha unto Jesus, Lord, if thou hadst been here, my brother had not died.

But I know, that even now, whatsoever thou wilt ask of God, God will give it thee.

Jesus saith unto her, Thy brother shall rise again.

Martha saith unto him, I know that he shall rise again in the resurrection at the last day.

Jesus said unto her, I am the resurrection, and the life: he that believeth in me, though he were dead, yet shall he live:

And whosoever liveth and believeth in me shall never die. Believest thou this?

She saith unto him, Yea, Lord: I believe that thou art the Christ, the Son of God, which should come into the world.
(John 11:20-27)

Then when Mary was come where Jesus was, and saw him, she fell down at his feet, saying unto him, Lord, if thou hadst been here, my brother had not died.

When Jesus therefore saw her weeping, and the Jews also weeping which came with her, he groaned in the spirit, and was troubled.

And said, Where have ye laid him? They said unto him, Lord, come and see.

Jesus wept.

Then said the Jews, Behold how he loved him!

And some of them said, Could not this man, which opened the eyes of the blind, have caused that even this man should not have died?

Jesus therefore again groaning in himself cometh to the grave. It was a cave, and a stone lay upon it.

Jesus said, Take ye away the stone. Martha, the sister of him that was dead, saith unto him, Lord, by this time he stinketh: for he hath been dead four days.

Jesus saith unto her, Said I not unto thee, that, if thou wouldest believe, thou shouldest see the glory of God?

Then they took away the stone from the place where the dead was laid. And Jesus lifted up his eyes, and said, Father, I thank thee that thou hast heard me.

And I knew that thou hearest me always: but because of the people which stand by I said it, that they may believe that thou hast sent me.

And when he thus had spoken, he cried with a loud voice, Lazarus, come forth.

And he that was dead came forth, bound hand and foot with graveclothes: and his face was bound about with a napkin. Jesus saith unto them, Loose him, and let him go.

(John 11:32-44)

In your situation, things may look bleak. Things may look as though there is no hope left. Things may appear dead and now they may even stink.

But the One who created everything still sits on His throne. He is the Life and the Resurrection. There is always hope in the power and authority of Jesus.

He is EL SHADDAI: The All Sufficient God.

He is JEHOVAH-JIREH: The Lord Will Provide.

He is JEHOVAH-ROPHE: The Lord Who Heals.

He is JEHOVAH-SHALOM: The Lord Our Peace.

So speak the Word only! I said speak the Word only and only believe!

Only believe!

Chapter Eight

Where Does Sickness & Disease Come From?

Way back in the Garden of Eden, Adam and Eve walked in perfect, divine health! There was NO sickness and NO disease on the earth. Not only did they walk in complete PHYSICAL health, they also walked in complete SPIRITUAL health!

They walked by faith and not by sight. Their spirits ruled their intellect or their mind. Their minds were pure and innocent. They knew nothing evil. In fact, they didn't even know they were naked!

This was back when God was God of the world. All animals, spiders, wasps, snakes and all living things were tame and didn't bite or sting. There were no thorns, thistles or weeds. There were no earthquakes, no floods, no lightning, no tornados, no hurricanes, no tsunamis, no volcanoes and no avalanches.

All nature was in perfect harmony created by a perfect God. Perfect man and perfect woman were given dominion or authority over the perfect earth.

But when the devil convinced Adam and Eve to sin by eating the fruit from the *Tree of Knowledge*, several things happened.

First of all, since they ate the fruit from the *Tree of Knowledge,* their intellect or mind was elevated above their spirit. They no longer walked with God.

They now walked by sight and not by faith. Their five senses (seeing, hearing, smelling, tasting and feeling) ruled their mind and their spirit.

Secondly, satan became the god of this world and billions of demons invaded the earth. Wild beasts, snakes, spiders, wasps and other creatures became vicious. Earthquakes and other so-called natural disasters began because the earth was cursed due to the fall of man.

Thorns, thistles, weeds and other nuisances became a reality and the whole earth groaned because of Adam and Eve's sin.

Along with satan and his demons came sickness and disease. This was all part of the curse of the law. Remember, there was NO sickness and disease BEFORE satan became god of this world. Sickness and disease comes from satan, NOT God!

> He that committeth sin is of the devil; for the devil sinneth from the beginning. For this purpose the Son of God was manifested, that he might destroy the works of the devil. (I John 3:8)

In John 10:10, Jesus said:

> The thief (the devil) cometh not, but for to steal, and to kill, and to destroy: I am come that they might have life, and that they might have it more abundantly.
> (John 10:10)

How does the devil steal, kill and destroy?

He steals your joy and happiness if you are sick. He steals money you would use for food and clothing and now you must use it to buy medicine and pay doctors. He steals your peace and rest because your body is racked with pain or perhaps you must wait on a sick spouse or child.

The devil kills by bringing sickness and disease to a loved one or yourself. If left unchecked, the disease spreads until it destroys the entire body.

Are these hideous, horrible diseases, pains and suffering... are they from God? A million times NO! Sickness and disease are part of the curse of the law due to the fall of man and are the works of the devil... the new god of the world!

Deuteronomy 28:59-61 says:

> If thou wilt not observe to do all the words of this law that are written in this book, that thou mayest fear this glorious and fearful name, THE LORD THY GOD;
>
> Then the LORD will make thy plagues wonderful, and the plagues of thy seed, even great plagues, and of long continuance, and sore sicknesses, and of long continuance.

> Moreover he will bring upon thee all the diseases of Egypt, which thou wast afraid of; and they shall cleave unto thee.
>
> Also every sickness, and every plague, which is not written in the book of this law, them will the LORD bring upon thee, until thou be destroyed. (Deuteronomy 28:59-61)

Now, you must know that God does NOT bring sickness or disease upon a person. God is love. There is NO sickness or disease in Heaven. In the verses above, the words 'will make' and 'bring' actually mean, 'permit'. In other words, the Lord takes His hand of protection away and the devil attacks you with sickness and disease.

Notice the words 'every sickness and every plague'... that means EVERY sickness and EVERY disease including cancers, tumors, heart disease, migraine headaches, backaches, ulcers, high blood pressure, aids, mad cow disease, bird flu disease, and EVERY sickness and disease known or unknown to man.

But, praise God, Galatians 3:13 declares:

> Christ hath redeemed us from the curse of the law, being made a curse for us: for it is written, Cursed is every one that hangeth on a tree.   (Galatians 3:13)

I've read somewhere that in the old Roman Empire, when they annulled or cancelled a law, they wrote the law on a piece of wood and nailed it to a tree.

The act of nailing it to a tree meant that particular law was done away with or abolished forever. The word 'abolish' means, 'put an end to' or 'bring to an end' or 'do away with'.

So when the Bible says, *Cursed is every one that hangeth on a tree...* when Jesus was nailed to the tree, the curse of the law was done away with for those who are Christians... IT ENDED THERE AT CALVARY!

Point your finger with authority at the curse, at the sickness, at the disease in your body or in the body of a family member and say, *"No more! The curse in my family stops here!"*

"In the Name of Jesus, I break the curse of the law. I bind the demonic curse and cast it out in the Name of Jesus. I plead the precious shed blood of Jesus over my family. And I command these curses to stop in my family once and for all in the Name of Jesus!"

Praise God! Jesus has redeemed us from the curse of the law! Therefore we are NOT subject or under authority to ANY kind of sickness and disease! In fact, by the victory won by Jesus on the cross and by us being born again and being a child of God, WE have authority in the Name of Jesus over sickness and disease and they MUST leave when we command them to do so in Jesus' Name!

The more you know and understand about sickness and disease, the better you can stand against them and overcome them in the Name of Jesus. There are FIVE ways in which sickness and disease attack us.

We have just studied the first one... that when we SIN and fall out of fellowship with the Father and His Son, Jesus, this opens the door for satan to inflict us with sickness and disease. But if we truly repent of our sin, we can expect to be completely healed by asking the Lord to heal us.

> And WHATSOEVER ye shall ask in my name, that WILL I DO, that the Father may be glorified in the Son.
> If ye shall ask ANY THING in my name, I WILL DO IT.   (John 14:13-14)

One reason that some children are born with birth defects is the mother using drugs, tobacco and/or alcohol while being pregnant. Of course this is sin with the result being sickness and disease to the child and eventually to the mother.

The second way in which sickness and disease attack us is through GENERATIONAL CURSES. In fact, this is the main cause of children being born sick, diseased and afflicted. It's also the main cause of why so many people are sick.

People say, *"I inherited bad genes"* or *"cancer runs in my family"* or *"heart disease runs in my family"* or *"everybody in my family has high blood pressure"*.

The truth is they are living under a generational curse!

> I the LORD thy God am a jealous God, visiting the INIQUITY OF THE FATHERS UPON THE CHILDREN unto the THIRD AND FOURTH GENERATION of them that hate me.   (Exodus 20:5)

The unrepentant sins committed by a great, great grandfather or by a great, great grandmother 100 years ago may be the cause of your sickness or disease today!

Just as you may pass down a family heirloom, you may also have a family DEMON that is passed down from generation to generation! Demons are spiritual so they don't die. They are thousands or maybe millions of years old!

When a demonic spirit of cancer (or some other disease) kills one family member, the demon leaves their body and invades another family member's body and kills them... and so forth from generation to generation. This is a generational curse.

But praise God generational curses can be stopped! Demons can be cast out! In Mark 16:17-18, Jesus said:

> And these signs shall follow them that believe. IN MY NAME SHALL THEY CAST OUT DEVILS; they shall speak with new tongues;
>
> They shall take up serpents; and if they drink any deadly thing, it shall not hurt them; THEY SHALL LAY HANDS ON THE SICK, AND THEY SHALL RECOVER.
> (Mark 16:17-18)

The Bible says that ANY believer should be able to cast out demons and heal the sick! A believer means a 'believing one' or a Christian. Notice that the Scripture says, 'SHALL' and NOT 'maybe or sometimes'! This should be an everyday normal occurrence for someone who understands their authority in Jesus and knows how to use the Name of Jesus in dealings with demons!

The third way that sickness and disease attack us is by the food we eat and by the air we breathe.

If you could see into the spirit realm, you would see the air around you literally infested with demons! The spirit world is JUST AS REAL as the natural world or the world in which we live!

I don't mean to frighten you. I'm simply trying to help you understand how sickness and disease attack us. We shouldn't be frightened of demons anyway because of what Jesus has done. WE are THEIR MASTER in the Name of Jesus! Demons are scared of believers who know who they are in Christ and who exercise their authority they have in Christ!

Now listen closely. When you breathe in the air around you, you can't help but breathe in microscopic viruses and germs. That's how you come down with colds or the flu. Viruses and germs are demonic in nature because they are sent by satan to invade the body to kill and destroy!

Viruses and germs are ALIVE! If you look at them under a microscope, you can see them wiggling around. Once they are inside a body, they live, breathe and GROW and make you sick. Some of them persist until they kill the body!

For example, cancer begins as a microscopic germ, a live demonic seed sent by satan. As long as the cancer is living or has life, it continues to grow and continues to destroy the body until it kills the body.

Even though the cancer seed is spiritual in origin, it causes PHYSICAL EFFECTS on the body!

But when the LIFE of the cancer is CAST OUT in the Name of Jesus, the physical effects of the cancer on the body soon return to normal and you are healed!

That's why doctors use radiation treatments on cancer patients. They are trying to kill the LIFE of the cancer. But in trying to kill the life of the cancer, radiation produces harmful effects on the body in other ways. But the LIFE of the cancer can be CAST OUT in the Name of Jesus by a believer and the patient can fully recover without radiation.

Also, some of the food we eat contains demonic germs that grow into diseases. Do you remember when Jesus cast out the legion of demons (Mark, chapter 5 and Luke, chapter 8) and allowed them to enter about 2,000 pigs?

Understand that demons are spirits without bodies. Without the faculties of a body they cannot talk or express themselves. In Matthew 12:43 Jesus said:

> When the unclean spirit is gone out of a man, he walketh through dry places, seeking rest, and findeth none.
> (Matthew 12:43)

They very much desire to enter into and live in people so they can express themselves through the person's bodily facilities. Some people give demons doorways to enter in by sinning in some way. The deeper a person sins and the more a person sins, the better a demon can gain control of the body. A person dealing in the occult or a person taking illegal drugs, etc., can eventually become demon possessed.

Demons are to blame for all of our crime today. They influence people to murder, to steal, and to commit acts of evil. Some people claim they hear voices inside their head... that's demons talking to them (using the person's bodily faculties)... persuading them to commit acts of violence.

The legal system tries to deal with the person, when in reality we should deal with the demon inside the person and cast it out! Then, the person will be gentle, kind and a good citizen!

The same problem persists in insane asylums. These people are not crazy. Many are demon possessed! Yet, the doctors and therapists try to deal with the person when they should be dealing with the demon inside the person! That's the only way a person can be cured or be made whole.

Now if demons can't find a human body to enter in, the next best thing is an animal. That's why some wild beasts attack, that's why some animals go mad... they are demon possessed! Remember, when Jesus cast out the legion of demons in Mark, chapter 5 and they went into the 2,000 pigs... the pigs went mad, ran down a hill into the sea and drowned! They became demon possessed!

During the 1,000 Year Millennium Reign of Christ on earth, the devil will be bound. During that time, there will be NO sickness and NO disease. ALL animals will be tame. There will be NO crime. There will be NO war. People will live to be very old. It was the same before Adam and Eve sinned. This PROVES that all sickness, disease, sin and evil are the work of the devil!

Since demons can live in or possess animals, some demonic germs or diseases can enter our food supply and subsequently into what we eat. That's why it's extremely important that we bless our food before we eat it. By blessing our food, demonic germs and viruses leave because they can't stand in the presence of God. And when you pray over the food you eat, it brings God on the scene and your food is sanctified!

Where Does Sickness & Disease Come From?

Even secular scientists have a clue that something is up but they don't really understand. They say to eat less red meat and more fruits and vegetables. God said basically the same thing in Leviticus, Chapter 11. However ALL food is good and clean if it is blessed before you eat it.

> For every creature of God is good, and nothing to be refused, if it be received with thanksgiving:
> For it is sanctified by the Word of God and prayer. (I Timothy 4:4-5)

But, if a demonic virus or germ does attack your body, the LIFE of the disease can be cast out in the Name of Jesus and the body returns to normal and is healed.

The fourth way that sickness and disease attack us is that God may allow it so He may be greatly glorified when you are healed.

> Now a certain man was sick, named Lazarus, of Bethany, the town of Mary and her sister Martha.
> (It was that Mary which anointed the Lord with ointment, and wiped his feet with her hair, whose brother Lazarus was sick.)
> Therefore his sisters sent unto him, saying, Lord, behold, he whom thou lovest is sick.
> When Jesus heard that, he said, This sickness is not unto death, but FOR THE GLORY OF GOD, that the Son of God might be glorified thereby. (John 11:1-4)

Jesus allowed Lazarus to die so He would be greatly glorified when He raised Lazarus to life again. Since Jesus made that statement, some people say, *"I am glorifying God in my sickness"*.

Listen... you are NOT glorifying God in your sickness... you are glorifying the DEVIL! The devil made you sick... NOT God! God may allow the devil to attack you but God receives glory when you are HEALED... NOT when you are sick!

Other people say, *"It may not be God's will to heal me"*.

This is as far from the TRUTH as you can get. To say that is actually an insult because Jesus took upon himself YOUR sickness or disease and SUFFERED with it so YOU may be HEALED! Proof is given in the next chapter.

To discover God's WILL in healing you, read the following Scripture:

> When he (Jesus) was come down from the mountain, great multitudes followed him.
> And, behold, there came a leper and worshipped him, saying, Lord, if thou wilt, thou canst make me clean.
> And Jesus put forth his hand, and touched him, saying, I WILL; BE THOU CLEAN. And immediately his leprosy was cleansed.   (Matthew 8:1-3)

Jesus stated His will. When the leper asked to be healed, Jesus said, *I WILL... be thou clean.* Acts 10:38 says:

> How God anointed Jesus of Nazareth with the Holy Ghost and with power: who went about doing good, and HEALING ALL that were oppressed of the devil.
> (Acts 10:38)

In the Scripture above, notice that Jesus healed ALL! Notice also that it is the DEVIL who makes people sick... NOT God!

In Luke 13:16, Jesus said:

> And ought not this woman, being a daughter of Abraham, WHOM SATAN HATH BOUND, lo, these eighteen years, be loosed from this bond... (Luke 13:16)

Make no mistake about it. It IS God's will for you to be healed!

The fifth way that sickness and disease attack us is that you may NOT know who you are or what you are in Christ. You may not know your legal rights in the family of God. You may not know the extent of victory that Jesus won for you on the cross.

And since you may not know who you are in Christ, the devil can inflict you with sickness and disease and keep you in bondage. This topic is so important that I have devoted an entire chapter later in this book about who you are in Christ.

Chapter Nine

Understanding Sickness

> Surely he both borne our griefs, and carried our sorrows: yet we did esteem him stricken, smitten of God, and afflicted.
>
> But he was wounded for our transgressions, he was bruised for our iniquities: the chastisement of our peace was upon him; and WITH HIS STRIPES WE ARE HEALED.
>
> All we like sheep have gone astray; we have turned every one to his own way; and the Lord hath laid on him the iniquity of us all. (Isaiah 53:4-6)

When we say that by His stripes we are healed, people visualize in their mind the physical stripes on Jesus' back.

But it goes much deeper than that… because sickness is SPIRITUAL… NOT physical!

Sure, the symptoms are manifested in the flesh but the actual sickness is spiritual! Remember, viruses and germs are demonic in nature. They are alive. They live and grow inside your body. They are demonic spirits sent by satan to kill and destroy.

The demonic disease inside your body causes PHYSICAL effects upon your body. That's why many doctors become baffled in trying to fight diseases. That's why many medications won't work. That's why radiation and many drugs produce harmful side effects while the disease continues to grow.

The problem is: Doctors are trying to deal with the PHYSICAL effects of the body when the root of the sickness is SPIRITUAL. And the majority of doctors have no clue on how to deal with spiritual diseases.

Since sickness and disease are spiritual in origin, God had to deal with them spiritually. God not only laid your sin upon Jesus (Jesus actually BECAME sin), but God also laid your sickness and disease upon Jesus because sin and sickness both come from the same source... satan.

Again, this proves that we have a two-fold or DOUBLE redemption... saved from sin AND saved from sickness... OR healed of sin AND healed of sickness... because BOTH sin and sickness are SPIRITUAL and by God laying YOUR SIN and YOUR SICKNESS upon Jesus... provision was made for YOU to receive BOTH!

All you need to do is ACCEPT it, ACT on it and PRAISE God for it!

It says in Psalm 34:20:

> **He (Jesus) keepeth all his bones: NOT ONE OF THEM IS BROKEN. (Psalm 34:20)**

And it says in John 19:33-36:

> But when they came to Jesus, and saw that he was dead already, THEY BRAKE NOT HIS LEGS:
>
> But one of the soldiers with a spear pierced his side, and forthwith came there out blood and water.
>
> And he that saw it bare record, and his record is true: and he knoweth that he saith true, that ye might believe.
>
> For these things were done that the scripture should be fulfilled, A BONE OF HIM SHALL NOT BE BROKEN.
> (John 19:33-36)

BUT...

The Bible says in 1 Corinthians 11:23-24:

> That the Lord Jesus the same night in which he was betrayed took bread:
>
> And when he had given thanks, he brake it, and said, Take, eat: this is my body, WHICH IS BROKEN FOR YOU:
> (1 Corinthians 11:23-24)

Now, you know that one Scripture can NOT contradict or disagree with another Scripture... that ALL Scriptures MUST AGREE!

However, of what we have just read, one Scripture says that *not one of His bones were broken* and another Scripture says, *this is my body which is broken for you.*

How do you explain this?

EASILY!

Jesus' bones were NOT PHYSICALLY broken by the Roman soldiers.

However...

Jesus' SPIRIT was broken by the SPIRITUAL STRIPES God laid on Him... for our iniquity and for our sicknesses and diseases... in which...

YOU CAN RECEIVE BOTH SALVATION AND HEALING IF YOU ONLY BELIEVE!!

Chapter Ten

Mustard Seed Faith

You may say, *"I understand your teaching and I do believe the Bible but my problem is FAITH... I need more faith!"*

So, HOW do you get more faith? Romans 10:17 says:

> So then faith cometh by hearing, and hearing by the word of God.
> (Romans 10:17)

So if faith comes by hearing the Word of God, let's hear what God's Word says!

In Matthew 17:20, Jesus said:

> If ye have faith as a grain of mustard seed, ye shall say unto this mountain, Remove hence to yonder place; and it shall remove; and nothing shall be impossible unto you. (Matthew 17:20)

Matthew 17:20 is a great Scripture! It's also one of the most misunderstood and misinterpreted Scriptures in the Bible!

All my life I have heard preachers and Bible scholars say that if we have faith the SIZE or as SMALL as a mustard seed, we could move mountains!

Listen carefully...

A mustard seed is the SMALLEST of all seeds. It is barely visible. It is only a SPECK! Some people wear mustard seed necklaces (with the seed encased in acrylic or enhanced with magnification because it is so small) to show their great mustard seed faith.

I'm sorry to have to tell you this, but if you have faith the SIZE of a mustard seed, YOU DON'T HAVE ANY FAITH AT ALL!

Is a SPECK all the faith you can come up with? And do you expect THAT to move mountains? Really... think about it!

Yes, people have been misunderstanding and misinterpreting Matthew 17:20 for years and years!

You may be scratching your head and asking: *"What are you talking about?"*

I'm talking about having faith AS a grain of mustard seed! You see, a mustard seed's faith says:

"I may be a tiny insignificant nothing and the SMALLEST of all seeds, but MY GOD SAYS that one day I'm going to be the LARGEST herb in the garden, even becoming a TREE and HAVE BRANCHES, where the birds will come and nest!"

We should speak the same language as the mustard seed.

"Yes, I may look in the mirror and see my feeble and diseased stricken body and pain may be tormenting me, and doubt, fear and worry may try to creep into my mind, but PRAISE GOD, I know, that I know, that I know, that I will soon become healthy, strong and walk in perfect health because BY JESUS' STRIPES I AM HEALED! GOD SAID IT, I BELIEVE IT AND THAT SETTLES IT!"

Since Exodus 15:26 says, *I am the Lord that healeth thee,* …then praise God, He is the Lord who <u>HEALS ME</u>!

Since Isaiah 53:5 says, *with his stripes we are healed*, … then praise God, by Jesus' stripes, <u>I AM HEALED</u>!

Since John 14:14 says, *If ye shall ask anything in my name, I will do it,* … then praise God, I can ask <u>ANYTHING</u> in Jesus' Name and <u>HE WILL DO IT</u>!

Since Mark 11:24 says, *What things soever ye desire, when ye pray, believe that ye receive them, and ye shall have them,* … then praise God, <u>WHATSOEVER</u> I desire, as I am praying, if <u>I BELIEVE</u> that I will receive them, <u>I SHALL HAVE THEM</u>!

Since II Timothy 1:7 says, *For God hath not given us the spirit of fear; but of power, and of love, and of a sound mind,* … then praise God, I do <u>NOT</u> have the spirit of fear but <u>I DO HAVE</u> a spirit of <u>POWER</u> and of <u>LOVE</u> and of a <u>SOUND MIND</u>!

Since I John 4:4 says, *greater is he that is in you, than he that is in the world,* … then praise God, <u>GREATER IS HE</u> that is <u>IN ME</u> than he that is in the world!

Since Luke 10:19 says, *I give unto you power to tread on serpents and scorpions, and over all the power of the enemy: and nothing shall by any means hurt you,* … then praise God, HE HAS GIVEN ME POWER to tread on serpents and scorpions and OVER ALL THE POWER of the enemy and NOTHING will hurt ME in ANY way!

Since Joshua 1:5 says, *I will be with thee: I will not fail thee, nor forsake thee,* … then praise God, He IS with ME, He will NOT fail ME and He will NOT forsake ME!

Since Deuteronomy 28:13 says, *the Lord shall make thee the head and not the tail; and thou shalt be above only, and thou shalt not be beneath,* …then praise God, I AM the HEAD and NOT the tail and I AM ABOVE ONLY and will NOT be beneath!

Since Philippians 4:19 says, *my God shall supply all your need according to his riches in glory by Christ Jesus,* … then praise God, my God WILL SUPPLY ALL MY NEED according to His riches in glory by Christ Jesus!

Since Isaiah 54:17 says, *No weapon that is formed against thee shall prosper,* … then praise God, NO weapon formed against ME shall prosper!

Since Jeremiah 29:11 says, *I know the thoughts that I think toward you, saith the Lord, thoughts of peace, and not of evil, to give you an expected end*, … then praise God, I KNOW that God thinks about ME with thoughts of PEACE and NOT evil, to give ME an expected end or HOPE in MY latter end!

Mustard Seed Faith believes not only the Word of God but also believes God OF the Word... that He will keep His promises and that He will perform His Word!

Mustard Seed Faith takes what God says LITERALLY and keeps standing on HIS WORD regardless of what you see or how you feel until God's healing power is manifested in your body! For II Corinthians 5:7 says, ... *we walk by faith, not by sight!*

Yes, there will be great fights with the demons of hell... it may look like you're getting worse instead of better... there may be great struggles in the middle of night... the pain may get worse before it gets better... you may think that the end is near...

BUT...

IF YOU <u>KEEP STANDING ON GOD'S WORD</u> AND DO NOT WAVER, DO NOT GIVE UP THE FIGHT, DO NOT GIVE IN TO NEGATIVE WORDS, DO NOT SUCCUMB TO DOUBT...

... BUT YOU <u>KEEP ON BELIEVING</u> AND <u>KEEP ON BELIEVING</u> AND <u>KEEP ON BELIEVING</u>.... THEN GLORY TO GOD... THE VICTORY <u>WILL</u> COME... THE VICTORY <u>WILL</u> BE YOURS!! PRAISE HIS HOLY NAME!!

Great faith is the product of great fights! Great testimonials are the outcome of great tests! Great triumphs can only come out of great trials! Every stumbling block must become a stepping stone and every opposition must become an opportunity to give God glory! Halleluiah!

Most people say that seeing is believing (like doubting Thomas). But Jesus says just the opposite... that <u>believing is seeing</u>!

In Matthew 9:22, Mark 5:34 and Luke 8:48, Jesus told the woman (who had the issue of blood), *<u>THY FAITH</u> hath made thee whole.*

In Matthew 9:29, Jesus told the two men (who had been blind), *According to YOUR FAITH be it unto you.*

In Mark 10:52, Jesus told Bartimaeus (who had been blind), THY FAITH *hath made thee whole.*

In Luke 17:19, Jesus told the man (who returned to give thanks and was one of ten lepers who were cleansed), THY FAITH *hath made thee whole.*

In Acts 3:16, Peter said that the lame man at the gate Beautiful was healed THROUGH FAITH *in Jesus' Name.*

In Acts 14:9, Paul said that the cripple from his mother's womb HAD FAITH *to be healed.*

I've heard some people say, *"Well, the Lord will heal me when he wants to."*

What these people who say this don't understand is that it's not up to the Lord to heal us (HE HAS ALREADY PROVIDED HEALING FOR US ON THE CROSS)... but...

... It is up to YOU to BELIEVE and ACT on what JESUS HAS ALREADY DONE!

You may be waiting for Jesus to act, when Jesus is waiting for YOU to ACT because He acted 2,000 years ago! Now, it's YOUR TURN!!

Act out your faith! Remember, you are saved by faith and you are healed by faith. But, James 2:20 says that *faith without works is dead.* James 2:14 says *what doth it profit, my brethren, though a man say he hath faith, and have not works?* James 2:22 says that *by works, faith is made perfect.*

By the way, 'works' is defined as 'an act' or 'actions' or a 'deed'.

If you have a bad back, have faith in God to heal you and then bend over and touch your toes <u>ACTING out your faith</u> while praising God!

If you have a bad leg, have faith in God to heal you and then run around the room <u>ACTING out your faith</u> while praising God!

Whatever the sickness or disease plaguing you, believe in God's healing power, claim your deliverance and then DO SOME KIND OF ACTION YOU COULD NOT DO BEFORE!

That's how you act out your faith!

And don't forget to PRAISE GOD for healing you! In fact, you should praise God for healing you <u>BEFORE</u> you see any change! Why? Because when you are praising God, you get your mind off your problem and put your mind on God. Many times, that's when healing takes place!

Consider this: The children of Israel at Jericho believed God and shouted while the walls were still UP! David believed and sang deliverance praises unto God while Saul was hunting him to KILL him! Paul and Silas sang praises to God even though they were CHAINED in prison!

The point I'm trying to make is: <u>shout the victory in the face of the devil</u>:

"Praise God, HEALING HAS BEEN PROVIDED FOR ME AND I ACCEPT IT NOW! God's Word says that

the truth will set me free. Now, I know the truth! With Jesus' stripes I AM HEALED!"

"I know that Jesus has redeemed me from the curse of the law! I know that Jesus has put ALL things under His feet! I know that at the Name of Jesus, EVERY knee must bow, of things in heaven, of things on earth, and things under the earth! I know that Jesus has given me a two-fold or double redemption so I can receive salvation and also, HEALING! GLORY TO GOD!"

Chapter Eleven

The Fig Tree

And on the morrow, when they were come from Bethany, he was hungry:

And seeing a fig tree afar off having leaves, he came, if haply he might find any thing thereon: and when he came to it, he found nothing but leaves; for the time of figs was not yet.

And Jesus answered and said unto it, No man eat fruit of thee hereafter for ever. And HIS DISCIPLES HEARD IT.
(Mark 11:12-14)

And when even was come, he went out of the city.

And in the morning, as they passed by, they saw the fig tree dried up from the roots.

And Peter calling to remembrance saith unto him, Master, behold, the fig tree which thou cursedst is withered away.

And Jesus answering saith unto them, HAVE FAITH IN GOD.

For verily I say unto you, That whosoever shall say unto this mountain, Be thou removed, and be thou cast into the

> sea; and shall not doubt in his heart, but shall believe that those things which he saith shall come to pass; he shall have whatsoever he saith.
>
> Therefore I say unto you, What things soever ye desire, when ye pray, believe that ye receive them, and ye shall have them. (Mark 11:19-24)

Jesus is hungry and He sees a fig tree covered with leaves. But when He gets to it, there are no figs! That's because, according to Mark 11:13, *the time for figs was not yet.*

So Jesus said to the tree… He SPOKE to the tree… He used <u>faith and spiritual authority and commanded</u> the tree to die and that fig tree died!

But listen carefully. When Jesus spoke to the fig tree, IT DIED INSTANTLY! However, the leaves were still green and pretty! But that didn't matter. The fig tree was dead.

If that had been us, we would have looked at that fig tree and STILL SEEING the green leaves, we would say, "I told you to die so die now in the Name of Jesus!"

Then STILL SEEING the green leaves, we would say, "I wonder why those leaves are not turning brown. Why isn't it working?"

THE TRUTH IS… When we spoke to the fig tree the first time in the Name of Jesus… it died. Remember, at the Name of Jesus, <u>every knee must bow</u> of things in Heaven and things in earth and things under the earth.

The fig tree is a thing. When we speak to it in the Name of Jesus and use faith and spiritual authority and command it to die it MUST die!

BUT... when we SEE with our eyes (which are one of our five senses) that the fig tree didn't wither INSTANTLY, we begin to DOUBT that the work was done... and ...

...listen carefully... when we speak to it a SECOND time... I said when we speak to it a SECOND time...

...the fig tree (which was already dead) is RESURRECTED to life again because of our unbelief that the work was done the first time! Read that again and again!

It's the same with sickness, disease, pain and demons. When we use faith and spiritual authority and command the life of that disease to leave in the Name of Jesus, the life of that disease is gone. Understand that it MUST leave! It has NO choice!!

If you are a true child of God with no unforgiven sin in your heart... and you know who you are in Christ and you exercise your rights as a believer... and you lay hands on a person in the Name of Jesus...

...and you use faith and spiritual authority to command the life of that disease to leave... <u>there is absolutely NO possibility of it remaining</u>. It absolutely has to leave!

But then... here is where we fail. You see, sickness and disease are SPIRITUAL in origin but they cause PHYSICAL effects on the body. Physical effects are called symptoms of the disease.

Listen carefully. When you cast out the life of the disease, and even though the life of the disease which caused those symptoms is NOW GONE… it takes a little while for the symptoms to go away and the body return to normal.

THAT'S THE PROCESS OF HEALING!

But if you allow yourself to walk by sight and not by faith… when you SEE or FEEL that the symptoms are still there… this makes many people DOUBT that the life of the disease has left and they command it to leave a second time.

And <u>when you command it a second time</u>, the life of the disease has ears (REMEMBER, IT IS SPIRITUAL IN ORGIN) and it now knows that you didn't really believe it would leave in the first place… and the life of that disease goes right back into the body from which it came!

Faith, spiritual authority and commanding goes together just like body, soul and spirit. When you meet the conditions… If you are a true child of God with no unforgiven sin in your heart…

…and you know who you are in Christ and you exercise your rights as a believer… and you lay hands on a person in the Name of Jesus…

…using faith and spiritual authority to command the life of that disease to leave… then there is absolutely NO possibility of it remaining. IT ABSOLUTELY HAS TO LEAVE! <u>IT MUST BOW TO THE NAME OF JESUS</u>!

If you absolutely without a shadow of a doubt believe that… then you WILL have the victory! So instead of commanding it to leave a second time, thank God and praise Him for the victory because the work was done the first time!

And that's the KEY to victory... PRAISE and THANKSGIVING with NO DOUBTING!!

Chapter Twelve

The Lord's Supper

> The Lord Jesus the same night in which he was betrayed took bread:
> And when he had given thanks, he brake it, and said, Take, eat: this is my body, which is broken for you: this do in remembrance of me.
> After the same manner also he took the cup, when he had supped, saying, This cup is the new testament in my blood: this do ye, as oft as ye drink it, in remembrance of me. (I Corinthians 11:23-25)

The Lord's Supper is Holy Communion and should be taken very seriously. In fact, the Apostle Paul tells us to examine ourselves and to make sure we are worthy to partake of the Lord's Supper (I Corinthians 11:27-30).

Jesus was serious about His suffering, crucifixion and death. He was serious about taking upon Himself OUR sin, OUR trespasses, OUR infirmities, OUR sicknesses, OUR diseases and becoming the Lamb of God, the ULTIMATE SACRIFICE... God's BEST... WITHOUT sin... WITHOUT blemish... for OUR SAKES!

The Lord's Supper was the point of NO return! Jesus was SEALING an OATH that He WOULD carry out the Father's will and plan to give us eternal life. The Lord's Supper was and still is no small matter. It was and still is a Holy Act of Jesus OFFERING HIMSELF TO US!

That's why, whenever you partake of the Lord's Supper, you MUST do it with complete REVERENCE and SINCERITY.

But, there's MORE to the Lord's Supper than many people think.

The BREAD signifies Jesus' body that was whipped, lashed and lacerated so YOU may be HEALED! The CUP signifies Jesus' Holy Blood that was shed so YOU may have FORGIVENESS and REMISSION OF SINS AS FAR AS THE EAST IS FROM THE WEST!

Once again, THIS PROVES THAT JESUS GAVE US A TWO-FOLD OR DOUBLE REDEMPTION... AND YOU CAN RECEIVE HEALING AS EASILY AS SALVATION... SIMPLY BELIEVE!

Some people receive healing while they are taking the Lord's Supper. Believe while you are taking and you can be healed also!

Don't wait for your church to have a communion service. There's nothing wrong with you having the Lord's Supper at your home... with your spouse or alone with the Lord!

Now think about YOUR sickness... YOUR disease being placed upon HIM by God... Jesus bearing YOUR sickness or disease... suffering not only how YOU are suffering right now... but Jesus suffering with

EVERYONE'S sickness and disease at the SAME TIME (everyone who has ever lived or who will ever live)... Jesus suffering with cancers, heart diseases, brain tumors, migraines, ulcers, leukemia, asthmas, emphysemas, and EVERY sickness and disease at the SAME TIME...

Now think about God literally CRUSHING Jesus' spirit with your iniquity... Jesus actually BECOMING SIN... yes, Jesus suffering not only physically but also spiritually... even crying out, *My God, my God, why hast thou forsaken me?* (Matthew 27:46)

Now think about with His stripes, He made provision for YOU to be healed... He took YOUR SICKNESS, YOUR DISEASE, YOUR PAIN, YOUR WEAKNESS UPON HIMSELF... He suffered with them in HIS body so you don't have to suffer with them in YOUR body... now, eat the BREAD, His flesh... His body... so YOUR body MAY BE MADE WHOLE! Halleluiah!

Now, take the cup and as you drink, think about the PRECIOUS SHED BLOOD OF JESUS... that without the shedding of blood there could be no remission of sin... that with HIS shed blood, provision has been made for YOUR salvation... provision has been made for YOU to have eternal life... that JESUS paid for YOUR sin IN FULL so you don't have to.

Now PICTURE HIM IN YOUR MIND... on the cross, with a bloody, mangled body, and with anguish and unbearable suffering, He says to YOU; *"My child, I love YOU... I died for YOU... I took YOUR sin upon ME... I took YOUR sickness upon ME... and since I bore it all for YOU... all YOU have to do to receive salvation and healing is to SIMPLY CONFESS ME AND BELIEVE ON ME... because <u>IT IS FINISHED!</u>"*

Now, picture in your mind, the resurrected and glorified CHRIST...

> ... wearing a long robe with a gold sash across His chest...
>
> His head and His hair white like wool, as white as snow... His eyes like a flame of fire...
>
> His feet like fine brass as if they burned in a furnace... and His voice thundering like mighty ocean waves...
> (Revelation 1:13-15 New Living Translation)

Then, He speaks:

> Fear not, I am the first and the last:
>
> I am he that liveth, and was dead; and, behold, I am alive forevermore, Amen; and HAVE THE KEYS OF HELL AND OF DEATH. (Revelation 1:17-18)

Brothers and sisters, when Jesus died on the cross, the provision for YOUR <u>salvation and YOUR healing WAS FINISHED</u>!

But Jesus went further! He went to hell, dethroned Satan... and *having spoiled principalities and powers, he made a shew of them openly, triumphing over them in it* (Colossians 2:15)... and Jesus repossessed the keys of hell and death that satan got with the fall of man in the Garden of Eden! Praise His Holy Name!

Now we can sing with joy:

> 0 death, where is thy sting? 0 grave, where is thy victory? (I Corinthians 15:55)

Chapter Thirteen

The Children's Bread

And, behold, a woman of Canaan came out of the same coasts, and cried unto him (Jesus), saying, Have mercy on me, 0 Lord, thou son of David; my daughter is grievously vexed with a devil.

But he answered her not a word. And his disciples came and besought him, saying, Send her away; for she crieth after us.

But he answered and said, I am not sent but unto the lost sheep of the house of Israel.

Then came she and worshipped him, saying, Lord, help me.

But he answered and said, It is not meet to take the CHILDREN'S BREAD, and to cast it to dogs.

And she said, Truth, Lord; yet the dogs eat of the crumbs which fall from their masters' table.

Then Jesus answered and said unto her, O woman, great is thy faith: be it unto thee even as thou wilt. And her daughter was made whole from that very hour.

(Matthew 15:22-28)

What did this Gentile woman say that made her faith so great?

She was saying, *"Lord, you have ALL AUTHORI7Y over ALL things. Why, even the WEAKEST part of you is MUCH GREATER than the greatest demon or the greatest disease! Even the SLIGHTEST touch or ONE word from you can shake Heaven, earth and hell! Even a CRUMB from you can cast out a demon!"*

This woman was seeking to have a devil cast out of her daughter but she was really seeking HEALING because the Scripture says, her daughter was MADE WHOLE... which means all, every whit, throughout, whole!

Therefore, Jesus was calling healing THE CHILDREN'S BREAD! Remember, the BREAD of the Lord's Supper signifies Jesus' body that was striped and beaten so YOU may be HEALED or BE MADE WHOLE!

But, you may say, *"Jesus was referring to the Jews as 'the children' in this Scripture. I am a Gentile. How does this Scripture apply to me?"*

Romans 11:17 says:

> ... and thou (Gentiles), being a wild olive tree, wert grafted in among them (Jews), and with them partakest of the root and fatness of the olive tree (Jesus);
> (Romans 11:17)

Romans 11:17 (New Living Translation) says it this way:

> And you Gentile, who were branches from a wild olive tree, were grafted in. So

> now YOU ALSO RECEIVE the blessing God has promised Abraham and his children, sharing in God's rich nourishment of his special olive tree.
> (Romans 11:17 New Living Translation)

Praise God! If you are born again, you are a child of God, grafted into His family and AS A REAL SON OR REAL DAUGHTER WITH ALL FAMILY PRIVILEGES, YOU ARE AT LIBERTY TO DINE AT GOD'S TABLE WITH A PLATE FULL OF THE CHILDREN'S BREAD!!

YOU DO NOT HAVE TO BEG FOR CRUMBS THAT FALL FROM THE MASTER'S TABLE!

IN HIS HOLY NAME, <u>ACCEPT YOUR HEALING AND DELIVERANCE NOW</u>!!

Chapter Fourteen

The Name Of Jesus

> Wherefore God also hath highly exalted him, and given him a name which is ABOVE EVERY NAME:
> That at the name of JESUS <u>every knee should bow</u>, of things in heaven, and things in earth, and things under the earth;
> (Philippians 2:9-10)

The NAME of Jesus is supreme. The NAME of Jesus has power. The NAME of Jesus has authority. In fact, the NAME of Jesus is just as POWERFUL as Jesus Himself! That's because His Name <u>represents</u> Himself. His Name <u>stands</u> for Himself.

When you use the NAME of Jesus in rebuking sickness and disease, <u>it's as though Jesus Himself is there doing it</u>! And you KNOW sickness and disease can NOT stand before Jesus for *he hath put ALL THINGS under his feet* (I Corinthians 15:27).

That's why Philippians 2:9-10 says that at the NAME of Jesus *<u>EVERY KNEE MUST BOW</u>* and that includes EVERY sickness... EVERY disease... EVERY demon... even satan himself!

Read all the healings and miracles Jesus did that is recorded in the four gospels. As you read, pay close attention at how sickness, disease and demons reacted when Jesus spoke to them. In fact, many demons were ready to cast themselves out when they saw Jesus because they knew what was coming!

James 2:19 says, ...*the devils also believe, and tremble.*

Yes, demons remember how Jesus came into their own house, dethroned satan, paralyzed him, reduced him to naught, made a show of him openly and triumphing over them in it! Yes, demons are scared to death of Jesus, and THEY KNOW they MUST bow to Jesus' Holy NAME!

Not only do demons know they must bow to Jesus' Name, but sickness, disease and EVERYTHING in Heaven, earth and hell KNOW they too, MUST bow to Jesus' NAME!

No wonder Jesus said in Mark 16:17-18:

> And these signs shall follow them that BELIEVE; In my NAME shall they CAST OUT DEVILS; they shall speak with new tongues;
> They shall take up serpents; and if they drink any deadly thing, it shall not hurt them; THEY SHALL LAY HANDS ON THE SICK, AND <u>THEY SHALL RECOVER</u>.
> (Mark 16:17-18)

Jesus didn't say that the sick might recover or maybe they would recover... Jesus said they SHALL recover... that means beyond a shadow of a doubt they WILL recover! Hallelujah! Remember, <u>God said it... you believe it... and that settles it</u>!

Ephesians 1:19-23 (New Living Translation) says:

> I pray that you will begin to understand the INCREDIBLE GREATNESS OF HIS POWER for US who believe him.
> This is the SAME MIGHTY POWER that raised Christ from the dead and seated him in the place of honor at God's right hand in the heavenly realms.
> Now HE IS FAR ABOVE ANY RULER OR AUTHORITY OR POWER OR LEADER OR ANYTHING ELSE IN THIS WORLD or in the world to come.
> And GOD HAS PUT ALL THINGS UNDER THE AUTHORITY OF CHRIST and he gave him this authority for the BENEFIT OF THE CHURCH.
> (Ephesians 1:19-23 New Living Translation)

This amazing Scripture says that God has given Jesus ALL authority over ALL THINGS for the benefit of the CHURCH! What benefit? The Church (Christians) should walk in VICTORY, not defeat! Our services should not be in preaching the Word only but also in demonstration of His awesome POWER (I Thessalonians 1:5).

Since Jesus said, *All power is given unto me in heaven and in earth* (Matthew 28:18), we should have healings and miracles in the church on a regular basis, demons being cast out, people receiving the Holy Ghost, people being set FREE of alcohol, tobacco and other sinful habits, with scores of sinners being saved as a result of God's awesome power! THIS SHOULD BE THE NORM FOR TODAY'S NEW TESTAMENT, VICTORIOUS CHURCH!

John 14:13 says:

> And whatsoever ye shall ask IN MY NAME, that WILL I DO, that the Father may be glorified in the Son. (John 14:13)

John 14:14 says:

> IF YE SHALL ASK ANY THING IN MY NAME, I WILL DO IT. (John 14:14)

You cannot make a stronger statement or a stronger promise than saying, *"I will"*. Jesus is giving us HIS PERSONAL GUARANTEE that if we ask ANYTHING in His Name, He will do it! Praise His Holy Name! Hallelujah!

Therefore, we know that we can ask the Father to heal us in the Name of Jesus and we WILL BE HEALED! All you need to do is SIMPLY BELIEVE and take God at His Word... because WHAT GOD SAYS, GOD DOES!

GOD SAID: Let there be light... AND THERE WAS light!

JESUS SAID: If you ask anything in my Name... I WILL DO IT!

WHAT GOD SAYS, GOD DOES!

You can take it for granted; if God said it... IT WILL COME TO PASS!

Chapter Fifteen

Who You Are In Christ

Many people don't receive healing and stay in bondage to sickness, disease and even poverty simply because they don't know WHO THEY ARE or WHAT THEY ARE in Christ. They don't know about satan's legal defeat. They don't know about their legal rights in the family of God.

Here's an illustration. Suppose you were fighting in a foreign country, captured by the enemy and imprisoned. A short time later, your army wins the war, liberates the country and sets the captives free.

Only the prison guard in the prison you are in doesn't tell you about it. You have been set free legally but you are still imprisoned because you don't know about your freedom from the enemy. You're held in bondage even though you are on the winning side.

Here's another illustration. Suppose that your bank wins a class action lawsuit on behalf of their depositors. You and every other depositor get a settlement of $100,000 automatically deposited into your bank checking account. However, since the bank didn't tell you, you know nothing about it.

But, the money is legally yours... it is in your account and it's there for you to withdraw and use at anytime you wish... but you still don't know anything about it. So even though it's yours, it's not doing you any good.

So there you are... worrying about how you're going to pay bills... about how you are going to buy food... about how you are going to pay the rent... when all the time... $100,000 is sitting in your bank account free and clear... for you to withdraw and use at any time you wish... but you simply don't know about it.

Now, just because you don't know about it, doesn't make this money have any less value. It's there... sitting there waiting for you to ACT on it... to USE it!

It's the same in real life. YOUR healing is sitting there... waiting for YOU to ACT on it... to USE it!

Jesus has set you free. He said, *if the Son therefore shall make you free, ye shall be free indeed* (John 8:36).

However, you are still living in bondage to sickness, disease and/or poverty because you don't know about your liberation from satan. But in a few minutes, you WILL know because I'm going to tell you!

It all began back in the Garden of Eden. Adam and Eve walked in perfect health until they sinned. God was the God of the world until man sinned. Then, satan became god of the world. After the fall of man, every sickness and disease came upon the people as part of the curse of the law.

Sickness and disease continued to run rampant on the earth until Jesus came to redeem mankind from sin, redeem mankind from the curse of the law (sickness and disease), to strip satan of his power and authority and restore man's relationship with God.

Therefore, since Jesus came and paid the price over 2,000 years ago for our disobedience and liberated us from satan's stronghold, we have been set FREE from sin, FREE from sickness, FREE from disease, FREE from pain, FREE from poverty, FREE from all bondage!

Colossians 1:13 says:

> Who hath delivered us from the power of darkness, and hath translated us into the kingdom of his dear Son: (Colossians 1:13)

When you are saved or born again, your spirit is translated in a micro-second out of the power of darkness or satan's kingdom into light or the Kingdom of God's dear Son. The satanic nature from the god of this world moves out... and God's nature from above moves in.

You go from being a child of the devil to being a child of God in a split second!

Now you can understand the Scripture that says you are not OF this world.

> ...ye are not of the world, but I have chosen you out of the world, (John 15:19)

II Corinthians 5:17 says:

> Therefore if any man be in Christ, he is a new creature: old things are passed away; behold, all things are become new.
> (II Corinthians 5:17)

The instant our spirit is translated, we become a NEW creature with NO past! You may look the same in the mirror but there is a <u>brand new person on the inside</u> of your body!

It's like if you move out of your house and another person moves in. The house still looks the same on the outside but there is a new person, a DIFFERENT PERSON living inside! The new person doesn't have to give account of the past life of what the other person did because they didn't do it. It was the other person that did those things!

Likewise, when your spirit is recreated and you become a new creature, all your sins are FORGIVEN and FORGOTTEN. If the devil tries to remind you of them, you can laugh and say, *"Devil, that was somebody else, not me! I'm a NEW person with NO past! Halleluiah!"*

Romans 8:14-16 says:

> For as many as are led by the Spirit of God, they are the sons of God.
> For ye have not received the spirit of bondage again to fear; but ye have received the Spirit of adoption, whereby we cry, Abba, Father.
> The Spirit itself beareth witness with our spirit, that we are the children of God:
> (Romans 8:14-16)

When your spirit is recreated and you become a new creature, your old nature is replaced with God's nature. You are now a citizen of Heaven and NOT of earth and you are NOT a servant, but a true <u>CHILD OF GOD</u>!

John 15:5-8 says:

> I am the vine, ye are the branches: He that abideth in me, and I in him, the same bringeth forth much fruit for without me ye can do nothing.
>
> If a man abide not in me, he is cast forth as a branch, and is withered; and men gather them, and cast them into the fire, and they are burned.
>
> <u>If ye abide in me, and my words abide in you, ye shall ask what ye will, and it shall be done unto you</u>.
>
> Herein is my Father glorified, that ye bear much fruit; so shall ye be my disciples.
> (John 15:5-8)

Galatians 3:26-29 says:

> For <u>ye are all the children of God by faith in Christ Jesus</u>,
>
> For as many of you as have been baptized into Christ have put on Christ.
>
> There is neither Jew nor Greek, there is neither bond nor free, there is neither male nor female: for <u>ye are all one in Christ Jesus</u>.
>
> And <u>if ye be Christ's, then are ye Abraham's seed, and heirs according to the promise</u>. (Galatians 3:26-29)

John 14:18-21 says:

> I will not leave you comfortless: I will come to you.
>
> Yet a little while, and the world seeth me no more; but ye see me: because I live, ye shall live also. At that day ye shall know

that <u>I am in my Father, and ye in me, and I in you</u>.

He that hath my commandments, and keepeth them, he it is that loveth me: and he that loveth me shall be loved of my Father, and I will love him, and will manifest myself to him. (John 14:18-21)

We are all ONE in Christ! He is the vine; you are one of the branches of the vine. Jesus is the head; you are part of His body. Jesus is the heir of God; you are a joint heir of God with Jesus!

Jesus is God's Son. You are God's son or daughter. Jesus is your Brother. You are in God's Royal family with ALL FAMILY RIGHTS AND PRIVILEGES!

Romans 8:17 says:

And if children, then heirs; heirs of God, and joint-heirs with Christ, (Romans 8:17)

Let's say that you and another person are joint heirs of $1,000.00. You do not own $500 each. <u>You both co-own the entire &1,000.00</u>. Likewise, you and every Christian are joint heirs with Christ! This means that you have the same family rights and the same family privileges that Jesus has!

Now we can understand the Scripture that says:

Verily, verily, I say unto you, He that believeth on me, <u>the works that I do shall he do also</u>; and greater works than these shall he do; because I go unto my Father.

> And <u>whatsoever ye shall ask in my name, that will I do</u>, that the Father may be glorified in the Son.
>
> <u>If ye shall ask any thing in my name, I will do it.</u>   (John 14:12-14)

This is because you are in Christ and Christ is in you. We are all ONE in Christ. He is the vine and you are one of the branches. The vine gives life to the branches but the FRUIT of the vine is produced on the BRANCHES!

You may be in this world but you are not of this world. You are a true child of God! You have been translated out of the authority of darkness into the kingdom of God's dear Son!

II Corinthians 5:20 says:

> Now then we are <u>ambassadors for Christ,</u>   (II Corinthians 5:20)

There is something special that ambassadors have that ordinary citizens of the country don't have… and that is…

DIPLOMATIC IMMUNITY!!

That means ambassadors are not under authority of the government in the country which they are living.

Since we are now citizens of Heaven means that the god of this world (satan) has NO dominion over you. He has NO authority over you. He cannot hold you in bondage. He has NO power over you.

You are not of this world but you are now a citizen of Heaven and sent by Jesus back into this world to become an ambassador for Him until He returns.

The devil is NOT your master. In the Name of Jesus, YOU are now HIS master! Sickness and disease has NO authority over you. In the Name of Jesus YOU now have authority over sickness and disease! Jesus has defeated them. They are YOUR servants. They MUST GO in the Name of Jesus!

Romans 8:11 says:

> But if the Spirit of him that raised up Jesus from the dead dwell in you, <u>he that raised up Christ from the dead shall also quicken your mortal bodies</u> by his Spirit that dwelleth in you.   (Romans 8:11)

What a Scripture! The SAME POWER that raised Jesus from the dead now lives in YOU! This power (the Holy Spirit) will quicken or HEAL your MORTAL BODY!

Now we can understand this Scripture:

> ...greater is he that is in you, than he that is in the world.   (1 John 4:4)

The sickness, disease, pain and poverty in this world are NO MATCH for the GREAT AWESOME POWER of the Holy Spirit living inside you! <u>Rise up and claim your deliverance NOW!</u>

Colossians 2:15 says:

> And having spoiled principalities and powers, he made a shew of them openly, triumphing over them in it.
>   (Colossians 2:15)

When Jesus defeated satan and stripped him of his power and authority, He didn't do it for Himself. He did it for us! But WE are credited with doing it! This is almost more than the human mind can comprehend!

We were crucified with Christ...

> ...our old man is crucified with him, that the body of sin might be destroyed, (Romans 6:6)

And we were buried with Him...

> ...we are buried with him by baptism into death: (Romans 6:4)

And we were raised with Him...

> And hath raised us up together... (Ephesians 2:6)

And we sit with Him in Heaven...

> ...and made us sit together in heavenly places in Christ Jesus: (Ephesians 2:6)

Do you understand now that satan, sin, sickness and disease have NO dominion and NO authority over us... that in the Name of Jesus, WE are THEIR Master... that ALL THINGS have been put under our feet by Jesus... that we are MORE than conquerors through Jesus Christ!

Let's summarize...

Jesus has already provided healing for you... <u>Jesus bore your sickness 2,000 years ago and defeated it!</u>

You no longer have to bare sickness or disease in your

body... <u>you have been redeemed from the curse of the law</u>!

You are no longer subject to the god of this world... because <u>you are no longer a citizen of this world, but you are now a citizen of Heaven</u>!

Know the victory that Jesus won for you... <u>know that everything Jesus did was credited to you as though YOU did it</u>!

Jesus did not need to be saved or healed... we did... He did it all for us!

ACT on what you believe... ACTING IS BELIEVING and BELIEVING IS ACTING!

PRAISE the Lord for what He has ALREADY done... SIMPLY BELIEVE, ACT ON WHAT YOU BELIEVE and YOUR healing will be MANIFESTED in your body!

Chapter Sixteen

Your Words

Words. The words you speak have power. What you say has been coming to pass your entire life. You are, right now, in the middle of what you have been saying.

> For verily I say unto you, That whosoever shall say unto this mountain, Be thou removed, and be thou cast into the sea; and shall not doubt in his heart, but shall believe that those things which he saith shall come to pass; he shall have whatsoever he saith. (Mark 11:23)

Let's analyze this Scripture.

Whosoever... This is YOU or ME or anyone!

Shall SAY unto... or speak unto... *those things which he SAITH* (SAYS) *shall come to pass...* whatsoever he SAITH (SAYS).

Three times this Scripture talks about SAYING! You are to SAY or SPEAK to the mountain.

After you SAY or SPEAK to the mountain, believe that what you SAID to the mountain has already happened... not because you see the results, but simply because you SPOKE to it!

If you believe what you say and not doubt… then Jesus said you will receive... or have what you SAID to the mountain!

This MOUNTAIN… this is an analogy... a mountain is anything that is huge and a seemingly unmovable problem that has risen up in your life.

A mountain could be sickness, disease, poverty, addictions, anything that is keeping you from living your life to the full and keeping you from being a victor instead of a victim.

You may say, *"Brother Jerry, you don't know how big the mountain is in my life. It would take a mighty big bulldozer to move it!"*

You need to understand that you already have the world's largest bulldozer in your hands… the Word of God! The Word of God mixed with faith can move your biggest mountain… even one the size of Mount Everest!

Be thou removed, and be thou cast into the sea… SPEAK to the mountain… LISTEN MOUNTAIN (or whatever problem you are experiencing)… you get OUT of my body, or you get OUT of my life, or you get OUT of my way, and go jump into the lake!

And shall not doubt in his heart… no negative thoughts, no negative talk, and no doubting Thomas.

But shall believe… <u>having faith with a corresponding action</u>… because faith without works is dead or faith without action does not bring you anything!

He shall have… or YOU will have…

Whatsoever he saith... or whatever YOU said... whatsoever! I looked up the word 'whatsoever' in the dictionary and it means 'what on earth'... 'no matter what'... 'anything'!

Anything! Of course, we know that anything here means anything that is in line with the word of God such as the promises of God... and we know the Bible promises YOU salvation, healing, prosperity, protection, peace and more!

Isaiah 55:10-11 says:

> For as the rain cometh down, and the snow from heaven, and returneth not thither, but watereth the earth, and maketh it bring forth and bud, that it may give seed to the sower, and bread to the eater:
> So shall my word be that goeth forth out of my mouth: it shall not return unto me void, but it shall accomplish that which I please, and it shall prosper in the thing whereto I sent it. (Isaiah 55:10-11)

Now, to produce a harvest, you must have seed and water for the soil to produce. Good seed sown makes a demand on the earth and forces it to produce.

The principle is this... God's Word comes down from heaven the same as the rain comes down to water the earth and causes it to bring forth fruit. So His Word comes down to the earth, and it will accomplish that where-unto He has sent it!

God's principle, or His means of bringing that to pass, is SEEDTIME and HARVEST. You sow a seed, and you reap a harvest. Again, good seed sown makes a demand on the earth and forces it to produce.

Luke 8:11 says:

The seed is the word of God. (Luke 8:11)

The soil is the heart of man. God furnishes the seed for the sower. But YOU must sow them. The way you sow the Seed is by saying the Seed... the Word of God... God's Promises... and speak them in faith OUT LOUD.

For example, God gave us the Seed of healing and deliverance in Psalm 107:20:

He sent his word, and healed them, and delivered them from their destructions.
(Psalm 107:20)

God has sent His Word and healed them and delivered them. Notice it says He sent His Word and HEALED them and DELIVERED them! God believed the work was done when He sent His Word (the Seed). He did it for them and He did it for us. How did He do it for us?

According as his divine power hath given unto us (His divine power is His Word... it came by the Holy Spirit, for the Holy Spirit is the Author of the Word of God) all things that pertain to life and godliness.
Whereby are given unto us exceeding great and precious promises: that by these ye might be partakers of the divine nature,
(2 Peter 1:3-4)

In other words, through this principle, as the rain and snow that comes down from heaven and returns not but waters the earth and produces fruit... God says *so shall my word be that goeth forth out of my mouth: it shall not return unto me void, but it shall accomplish that which I please, and it shall prosper in the thing whereto I sent it.*

So you take the Seed or the Word of God and PLANT it in the soil or in your heart... then you WATER it by speaking God's promise out loud and by doing this again and again several times a day, eventually the Seed will sprout in the soil, spring forth and produce a harvest in your life!

If you say something long enough, you will eventually begin to believe it! And when you believe it, that's when the work will be done!

So when you speak the Seed or Word of God against your mountain of need, the Seed keeps putting pressure on the mountain until the mountain must give way to the Seed and the mountain is removed!

Jeremiah 23:29 says:

> Is not my word like as a fire? saith the Lord; and like a hammer that breaketh the rock in pieces? (Jeremiah 23:29)

By speaking the Word of God against the mountain in your life, it's like hitting it with a hammer (mountains are made of rock).

By hitting the rock (by speaking to the mountain in your life) time and time again, over and over with the Hammer (the Word of God), the rock will eventually break in pieces and be removed! Halleluiah!

Mark 4:26-28 says:

> And he said, So is the kingdom of God, as if a man should cast seed into the ground;
>
> And should sleep, and rise night and day, and the seed should spring and grow up, he knoweth not how.
>
> For the earth bringeth forth fruit of herself; <u>first the blade, then the ear, after that the full corn in the ear.</u> (Mark 4:26-28)

You might say, *"I don't understand how speaking God's promises could change my circumstances."* <u>Jesus said you wouldn't understand it.</u> But He says in this Scripture to go to bed and get up. Surely you know how to go to bed and get up.

He means not to worry about it. You just simply SOW the Seed, WATER the Seed, go to bed, and get up. In other words, you exercise the power principle:

You sow the Seed by saying: *"Thank you Father for meeting my need. I'm proclaiming in Jesus' Name that there is abundance and no lack. I'll have the best job in town. I say it on the authority of the Word of God. I can have what I say, if I believe and not doubt in my heart. Whatever I do will prosper."*

Or...

You sow the Seed by saying: *"Thank you Father for sending your Word and healing me. For by Jesus' stripes I am healed. Thank you Holy Sprit within me for quickening and making alive my mortal body by your mighty and awesome power... the same power that raised Jesus from the dead. I say it on the authority of the Word of God. I can have what I say, if I believe and not doubt in my heart."*

Jesus said that you could have what you say, if you believe and not doubt in your heart!

>...for out of the abundance of the heart the mouth speaketh. **(Matthew 12:34)**

This Scripture means that YOU SAY what YOU BELIEVE. If you believe in your heart that *by His stripes you are healed*, you will talk healing and health instead of talking sickness and pain.

If you believe in your heart that *God shall supply all your needs* then you will talk having instead of talking lack.

Now, many times, people will speak from their head and not from their heart. For example, they may say, *"With His stripes I am healed"*. But five minutes later they say, *"If God doesn't hurry up and heal me, I don't know what I'm going to do"*.

The second confession nullified the first confession. <u>Your heart cannot believe two different things at the same time</u>. Therefore, one confession is coming from your heart and the other confession is coming from your head.

Now, this is very important! Whichever confession is coming from your HEART is the one you really believe and the one you will have! <u>If your heart and your words are not in agreement it will not work</u>! If you are living in sin, it will not work.

In this example, the confession, *"with His stripes I am healed"* is coming from the head because if you really believed that by His stripes you are healed, you wouldn't say the negative confession five minutes later!

> Thou art snared with the words of thy mouth, thou art taken with the words of thy mouth. (Proverbs 6:2)

The word 'snare' means 'trap' or 'noose'.

Some people say, *"I feel like I'm taking a cold"*. If you say that, guess what will happen?

You WILL have a cold! You say what you believe and you have what you say because you say what you believe... *out of the abundance of the heart, the mouth speaketh!*

Some people may eat something and later on feel sick. Now, instead of confessing God's Word over those demonic symptoms and in the Name of Jesus commanding the symptoms to leave... they say something like, *"I knew not to eat that because every time I eat that particular food it makes me sick"*.

And guess what? They WILL be sick! They made the wrong confession. They spoke the wrong words. They spoke sickness instead of speaking health.

> For by thy words thou shalt be justified, and by thy words thou shalt be condemned. (Matthew 12:37)

It's like accepting a package from the package delivery driver. The devil brings you a package (symptoms of sickness), you accept it (by saying you have it), then YOU HAVE the package (sickness) and the devil has the receipt (and laughing all the way)!

You can speak life or you can speak death.

You can speak sickness or you can speak health.

You can speak poverty or you can speak prosperity.

You can speak fear or you can speak God's protection.

You have what you say because you say what you believe and what you believe... you have!!

In the Old Testament, the father's verbal blessing upon the children was considered to be the greatest desire in the mind of the children. Why? Because words have power!

Words have power over your health and circumstances and over OTHER people's health and circumstances.

Some people are not aware of it but they are actually speaking curses over other people when they say things like, *"It looks like she won't make it"*... *"I heard that cancer runs in your family"*... *"You look so pale, something must be wrong with you"*... *"I'm sorry you're having such a hard time"*, etc.

People may mean well but they should dwell on the positive, not the negative, by saying: *"I'm praying and believing that the Lord will raise her up for His glory"*... *"I rebuke that generational curse over that family in the Name of Jesus"*... *"You look so well and vibrant"*... *"Praise God, I know things will be getting better for you"*.

Do you see the difference? Your words have power just as the Word of God has power.

Some people even speak curses over their children by saying things like, *"You'll never amount to nothing"*...

"You feel like you have a fever"... *"You'll probably grow up to be like your no good father"*... *"It sounds like you're coming down with a cold"*... *"If you don't wash your face, you'll have pimples"*... and on and on.

People also speak curses over themselves by saying things like, *"I nearly died laughing"*... *"I almost had a heart attack lifting that box"*... *"I can't believe I am so stupid"*... *"I almost broke my neck when I tripped"*... *"How crazy can I be"*... *"Now, I know I've lost my mind"*... *"Every time I cut myself, I nearly bleed to death"* ... and on and on.

IF YOU SAY these things, then YOU BELIEVE THEM and could actually bring these things into existence. So you must change your vocabulary at once and speak faith words, God's Words, life words. Because words have power whether you realize it or not and whether you believe it or not.

> **Death and life are in the power of the tongue: and they that love it shall eat the fruit thereof.** (Proverbs 18:21)

You can speak life or you can speak death. You can speak blessings or you can speak curses. It's your choice... but remember this: YOU HAVE WHAT YOU SAY!

A true story I've heard is that a man who had cancer was healed by the power of God. He was thankful every day but his wife didn't have faith. EVERY DAY she said: *"You better go see a doctor and have an operation before you die!"*... *"It's only a TEMPORARY relapse, I know you are still sick!"*... and many other things she told him.

In a few weeks, the cancer did come back and the man died. But, he was really and truly healed! What happened?

I believe that the WORDS his wife spoke over him everyday brought the cancer curse back upon him. You see, your ears are one of the gates to your soul. If you hear bad words and negative words and sick words long enough, eventually those words will take root into the person they are spoken to!

The man lost his healing by accepting his wife's words, even though she spoke them in love. <u>When he believed his wife's words more than God's Word</u>, the cancer came back and destroyed him!

He should have rebuked those words in the Name of Jesus and refused to even hear them! He should have also prayed for the Holy Spirit to illuminate the truth of God's Word into his wife's heart.

Yes, there will be great fights with the demons of hell... it may look like you're getting worse instead of better... there may be great struggles in the middle of night... the pain may get worse before it gets better... you may think that the end is near...

... BUT...

IF YOU KEEP STANDING ON GOD'S WORD AND DO NOT WAVER, DO NOT GIVE UP THE FIGHT, DO NOT GIVE IN TO NEGATIVE WORDS, DO NOT SUCCUMB TO DOUBT...

BUT YOU KEEP CONFESSING GOD'S WORD FROM YOUR HEART, AND YOU KEEP ON BELIEVING, AND KEEP ON CONFESSING, AND KEEP ON BELIEVING....

THEN GLORY TO GOD... THE VICTORY WILL COME... THE VICTORY WILL BE *YOURS*... PRAISE HIS HOLY NAME!!

Remember...

Great faith is the product of great fights!

Great triumphs can only come out of great trials!

Every stumbling block must become a stepping-stone and every opposition must become an opportunity to give God glory!

Halleluiah! Give Praise and Glory to His Holy Name!

Yes... you CAN receive healing as easily as salvation!

All you have to do is <u>SIMPLY BELIEVE and then ACT ON YOUR BELIEF</u>!

... the truth has now made you free! (John 8:32)

Chapter Seventeen

How To Keep Your Healing

> But he that received the seed into stony places, the same is he that heareth the word, and anon with joy recelveth it;
>
> Yet hath he not root in himself, but dureth for a while: for when tribulation or persecution ariseth because of the word, by and by he is offended. (Matthew 13:20-21)

Since sickness is caused by the devil, he will make an attempt to bring that sickness upon you once again.

Matthew 12:43-45 says:

> When the unclean spirit is gone out of a man, he walketh through dry places, seeking rest, and findeth none.
>
> Then he saith, I will return into my house from whence I came out; and when he is come, he findeth it empty, swept, and garnished.
>
> Then goeth he, and taketh with himself seven other spirits more wicked than himself, and they enter in and dwell there: and the last state of that man is worse than the first. (Matthew 12:43-45)

Why should you expect the Lord to heal you if you intend to keep on living in sin? Do you really expect the Lord to give you strength and health to continue doing the works of the devil?

However, the Lord is so good and so great that He does indeed heal sinners. But, once you have been healed, it is extremely important that you turn your entire life over to the Lord or you may lose your healing. If you are not saved, repent of your sin now and be baptized.

If you are currently not going to church, find a good Bible based church that teaches the truth of God's Word and attend regularly. Get involved in church activities.

It is critical to read your Bible DAILY... to soak in the Word of God. Cut out all the fifth and trash in your life. If you have bad habits, stop them in the Name of Jesus.

If old symptoms come back, rebuke them in the Name of Jesus. Don't believe the devil's lies. Don't even entertain the thought that you may not be healed. NEVER doubt your healing!

Re-read the previous chapter about the importance of the words that you speak. Never confess sickness or weakness. Don't listen to negative words from others.

Hebrews 4:14 says *let us hold fast our profession.* The word 'profession' is interpreted in the Greek dictionary as 'confession'. Therefore, hold fast to your confession that with His stripes you are healed!

If you hold fast your confession, the devil's test will pass and you will keep your healing! Then, go out and set others free in the mighty Name of Jesus!

Catalog of

Books, DVDs & Computer CDs

(All prices include shipping.)

Seven Seals Of Revelation Book – $20.00

Most of what you read and hear about end time prophecy either contains false doctrines or the timetables are out of order. That's because most people don't understand the Seven Seals of Revelation or don't realize the significance of them.

Most of the Book of Revelation that follows the opening of the Seven Seals (in Revelation, Chapter 6) details the secrets that the Seven Seals contain! Now, for the first time ever, the Book of Seven Seals has been un-sealed and you will discover the real truth about end time prophecy!

Words Of Life Book Volume 1 – $15.00

Powerful, faith-building messages as taught by Jerry Byler.

Titles include *Secrets To God's Power, Promotion Cometh, The New Math, Hope And A Future, Heaven,*

Three 'Friends' That You Can Do Without, Redeemed From The Curse Of The Law, Doing The Same Works As Jesus, How To Defeat Giants In Your Life, God Will Heal You, Two Kinds of Images, and The Total Package.

Words Of Life Book Volume 2 – $15.00

Powerful, faith-building messages as taught by Jerry Byler.

Titles include *The Secret To Healings And Miracles, Does The Devil Know Your Name?, Have Whatever You Say, Living An Abundant Life, Faith And Believing, Prayer, Faith And Righteousness, Whose Report Will You Believe?, In The Valley Of Dry Bones, As He Is So Are We In This World, The Potter's House, One In Christ,* and *Faith And Patience.*

Words Of Life Book Volume 3 – $15.00

Powerful, faith-building messages as taught by Jerry Byler.

Titles include *My Awesome Thursday Experience, 10 Steps To Spiritual Farming, What To Do When You Are Overwhelmed, Calling Things That Are Not As Though They Were, It Is Well, Fire of God, Keep On Asking, Destiny: Discovering Your Purpose In Life, The Power Of Binding And Loosing, The Gospel Train, Who You Are In Christ,* and *New Things.*

The 2 O'clock Diet Booklet - $7.00

Recently, I studied the lives of old-time healing evangelists in order to discover the secrets of their incredible power they all had in ministering to others. I discovered two key things they all did before they began their ministry that propelled them into a ministry of healings, miracles, signs and wonders.

As I implemented these two things in my life, I began to lose weight unexpectedly while still eating all of my favorite foods... without counting calories and without changing any food that I ate! In this powerful booklet, I share this incredible diet with others, that if followed, you can not only lose weight, but also perhaps launch you too into a ministry of healings, miracles, signs and wonders!

Supernatural Experiences DVD – $15.00

Discover the beauty, the serenity and peacefulness of Heaven... and the horror, the terror and the unquenchable fire of Hell...as eye witnessed and experienced by those who claim to have had out of body experiences! This is one of the best tools available to witness to lost loved ones and others who are unsaved.

Historic Revival and Evangelistic Magazines on Computer CD – $12.00 each

Here is a wonderful collection of early revival and evangelistic magazines in PDF files on Computer CD.

Hours and hours of interesting reading plus lots of pictures in most magazines!

The Voice Of Healing Computer CD – $12.00
45 issues in PDF Files, 1940s-1950s

The Pentecostal Evangel Computer CD – $12.00
26 issues in PDF Files, 1919-1955

The Alliance Weekly Computer CD – $12.00
50 issues in PDF Files, 1920-1946

The Latter Rain Evangel Computer CD – $12.00
52 issues in PDF Files, 1920-1946

Various Early Christian Magazines Computer CD – $12.00
45 issues in PDF Files, 1893-1919

Order Form

Note: All prices include shipping. All computer CDs contain one or more PDF files that opens with Adobe Acrobat - most computers have this software built in – if not, you can get it free here: http://get.adobe.com/reader/

Quantity	Title	Price Each
	Seven Seals Of Revelation Book	$20.00
	Words Of Life Book Volume 1	$15.00
	Words Of Life Book Volume 2	$15.00
	Words Of Life Book Volume 3	$15.00
	The 2 O'clock Diet Booklet	$7.00
	Supernatural Experiences DVD	$15.00
	The Voice Of Healing Computer CD	$12.00
	The Pentecostal Evangel Comp. CD	$12.00
	The Alliance Weekly Computer CD	$12.00
	The Latter Rain Evangel Comp. CD	$12.00
	Early Christian Magazines Comp. CD	$12.00

Total Amount Enclosed $_____

Print Your Name_____

Address_____

City_____ State_____ Zip_____

Please make checks and money orders payable to: Jerry Byler

Mail To:

Jerry Byler
PO Box 1618
Northport AL 35476

www.ingramcontent.com/pod-product-compliance
Lightning Source LLC
Chambersburg PA
CBHW071707040426
42446CB00011B/1956